Bible Bedtime Stories For Kids

A Collection of Relaxing Bible Stories to Help Your Children and Toddlers Go To Sleep While Learning Fundamental Christian Moral Values to Dream about all Night!

Ella Swan

Contents

1. The First Seven Days — 1

2. The Floating Zoo — 8

3. The Boy And The King — 17

4. The Baby On The River — 26

5. It's Raining Bread! — 35

6. Who Is Calling Samuel? — 43

7. In The Belly Of A Whale — 51

8. God's Chosen One — 61

9. The Night The Angels Sang — 69

10. Fishers Of Men — 78

11. Seeds In The Wind — 85

12. The Missing Sheep — 93

13. The Vineyard Workers — 102

14. The Kind Stranger — 108

15. The Man Who Left Home — 114

Final Words — 124

The First Seven Days

D id you know that during the first seven days of your life, you are just about as big as a grain of sugar? You're already made up of many tinier parts, though, that will make up all the bigger parts of you later on. It also takes seven days for most insect eggs to hatch and seven days for some baby plants to get their first leaves. Indeed, many wonderful things can happen in just seven days, and that's how long it took God to make the world we live in, too!

At the beginning of time, there was nothing, only God. There were no people. There wasn't a single plant or creature. There was no sound, not even the gentlest whisper of air. There wasn't a speck of light either.

"I can't see anything," God said as He sat in the endless darkness. "Is there any way I can get some light in here?"

And just like that, light appeared. It started out as a tiny white spark, then it turned into a golden flame. It got bigger and bigger, becoming a bright, burning ball. Then it burst like a balloon, the light inside it escaping to create such a huge splash.

God liked the light, but He also thought it was too bright to be there everywhere all the time, so He placed it in a giant jar. Whenever the light was in the jar, it was dark, and whenever the jar was opened, the light spilled everywhere, and everything was bright. To make it easier for the jar to open and close, too, God made two buttons that He could just press. He labeled the button to open the jar Day and the button to close the jar Night. Together, Day and Night combined to create one day.

This was the very first day.

Now that God had finished separating light and darkness and Day and Night, he decided to divide space. There was just too much space around Him, after all. God drew a great, big line, and He called the space above it Heaven.

Just like that, the second day was over.

As God sat in Heaven, He realized that there wasn't much to see. The space had been divided, but it was still empty, like a blank sheet of paper. So on the third day, God decided to make something. He created water from his fingertips and shaped it into a giant ball. It was beautiful! However, it looked too…blue and too clean.

"I think it needs a bit of dirt," God said.

So He created some dirt in the palm of His hand, and He placed smudges of it on the ball. He molded it into different shapes - some round, some long and thin, and some square but with rough edges. He also molded the surface of the land, making some parts higher and some parts lower. In this way, God made the mountains, hills, valleys, and plains. He also made steep cliffs and underground caves. God called the land Earth, and He called the waters around them Seas.

The ball was more pleasing to look at now, but it was still a little boring.

"It needs more color," God said. "It needs to come to life!"

God touched the Earth with the tip of His finger, and the Earth began to shake. Seeds formed deep inside the Earth, leaves sprouting from them to climb towards the surface and beyond. Some of these leaves became blades of grass covering the land. Some of them became plants that grew beautiful flowers of different colors, their sweet smell filling the air. Others grew taller and taller until they became trees with strong trunks and long branches. These branches grew even more leaves, and some grew their own flowers, too, which bloomed and turned into fruits of different shapes and sizes. These fruits had seeds of their own inside, too, so that new trees could grow.

God looked at the forests and the meadows and He smiled. Now, finally, His creation looked like a work of art. "That's more like it!"

And so day number three came to an end.

On the fourth day, God went back to His jar of light. He wanted to do something more with it.

"I want the light to bring out the beauty of the world I have made," He said.

He made a big ball of light to shine upon the world during the Day, to rise on one side and set on the other. It was like a spotlight shining down on everything from Heaven, painting the sky in different colors and making the flowers look even brighter.

Then God made a smaller ball of light to take over during the Night, giving the trees and the surface of the Seas a soft, silver glow. He made it so that it would keep changing its shape, sometimes looking perfectly round, sometimes smiling, and sometimes looking like someone had taken a bite out of it. Sometimes, it was even barely there at all.

Because there wasn't much light at Night, God also made smaller balls of flickering light like fairy lights across the dark sky. God placed some of them into groups, arranging the bright dots so that they could be connected to make pictures and tell stories. Then, He designed these groups of stars to take turns in the night sky so that they could not always be seen. In this way, the night sky would always look different, while the sky during the Day remained the same.

It was exactly how God liked it, and so He wrapped up the fourth day.

The next day, God looked once again at His masterpiece, trying to see what else He could add. It was colorful now, and it looked amazing, but there was still something missing.

"Maybe it needs more moving pieces," God said.

So God touched the Seas, and out of the water, whales jumped out, each creating a big splash. There were dolphins, too, and flying fish. Under the water, even more fishes appeared - big ones with sharp fins and teeth, ones with eight legs or arms, and others that looked like jelly. There were also plenty of small fishes that swam in groups. Some fishes were too lazy to swim and stayed buried in the sand, while the shy ones hid among the plants. There were also fishes that looked like leaves and some that were covered in spikes. Deep underwater, where the light could not reach, some fishes gave off their own sparkling lights, making it look like they were the audience in a concert.

The Seas were now full of life, but what about the sky?

"Let creatures appear in the sky," God said, and at once, the flapping of wings filled the air. Birds appeared, some huge and others small and fast. Some of them flew in groups, too, and made their own patterns in the sky, and some of them could sing and hold their own concert.

God was pleased. "Get along," he told the creatures. "Make this world your home and fill it with life."

This was the fifth day.

The next day, God turned His attention to the Earth. He touched the land, and animals appeared - tigers and monkeys in the forests, bears, wolves, and goats in the mountains, horses, deer, and rabbits racing across the meadows. Each animal was magnificent in its own way. Some were able to change colors. Others could produce different sounds. Some animals were experts at building their own homes.

God had fun watching these animals go about their day, and He thought, "It would be nice if there was someone to look after them."

So God created humans - a man and a woman who looked just like Him. Like Him, they had eyes to see the beauty of the world, hands to make things, minds to think of how they could make their lives better, and hearts to care for all of God's creation.

"I am putting you in charge of this world I have made," God told them. "Take care of it and fill it with even more life."

With that, the sixth day reached its end.

On the seventh day, God looked at everything He had made. Everything looked perfect, and He did not think there was anything left to add.

"It seems I am done with my work," He said. "So now, I will rest."

That is exactly what God did. After six days of creation, God put His head down and His feet up. It was a peaceful day, a blessed day, the perfect ending to the first seven days of how the world began.

The Floating Zoo

What do you do when it rains for weeks? Do you put on your boots and jump on puddles with the frogs? Do you stay inside and draw with your crayons or make a fort on your bed and camp with your toys? As for one man, he made a floating zoo - with God's help, of course.

For hundreds of years, God's creation filled the Earth. Babies were born, and they grew up to become mothers and fathers, having babies of their own. Families grew into clans and tribes, which settled in villages, towns, and cities. New animals were born, too. Baby birds, fishes, and platypuses called puggles hatched from eggs. The kangaroos had their joeys. The wolves and bats had their pups. The camels, elephants, and antelopes had their calves. New plants grew from the seeds inside fruits and flowers, sometimes with the help of humans.

Just as many plants in one place compete for sunlight and animals compete for food, the more humans there were, the less they got along.

The people started fighting - whether for food, for a place to sleep, for clothes, for jobs, or simple things like whose sheep ate whose grass or whose turn it was to bathe in the river. Some ended up stealing. Others did worse.

As people became cruel, the world began to suffer. Trees were cut down. Fields were burned. Animals were hurt or driven out of their homes, sometimes just for fun.

"The humans destroyed our nest today," a female dove complained tearfully to her husband. "Now, I don't know where to sleep or lay my eggs. I thought the humans were supposed to take care of us. Why do they keep doing bad things?"

"I don't know," the male dove answered. "But we'll just have to stay away from them. Even if they don't look after us, God will."

God was keeping His eye on everything, and He felt sad and angry to see what had become of everything He had made. "Maybe it was a mistake to create humans," He thought. "Because now, their minds and their hearts are full of evil, and they are destroying everything else I have made. If it was, then I have to make things right. I will make the world new and start all over again."

God thought about how He would do this, and He decided He would use water.

"I will send rains to wash away everything on Earth," God said. "And when it is over, the world will be clean and beautiful again, just like it was in the beginning, just as it should be."

God planned on washing away all humanity as well, but there was one good man whom He just could not bear to punish. His name was Noah, and by now, he was an old man - past six hundred years old, in fact. Still, he had lived well, praying often to God. He was also a good father to his three sons, Shem, Ham, and Japheth, and a caring husband to his wife. He was even kind to other people, even strangers and those who were not nice to him, and to all kinds of animals.

Because of this, Noah earned the favor of God, and so God said, "I will spare this man because even though other people have become cruel and selfish, he has remained good and faithful to me. I will spare his family, too, so that humanity will carry on and live good lives under his guidance."

One day, while Noah was gathering wood to make a fire, God spoke to him.

"Listen carefully, Noah," God told him. "I have seen how people's hearts have turned cold and how their evil ways have made the world a sad place to live in, so I will make the world new. I will send rains, and there will be a flood to wash away everything I have made."

Noah's eyes grew wide. "Everything?"

"Yes, except you and your family. You will be safe in a boat, which you will build exactly as I tell you."

Noah was glad to hear that he and his family would be saved, but there was something else that concerned him. "What about the animals, dear God? They, too, have done nothing wrong."

God paused for a moment, then said, "You may bring two of every kind of animal with you, but this means you will need a bigger boat. You will also need to store more food."

"Then I will do that," Noah said.

However, it was easier said than done. The boat Noah had to build was very big, after all, and he only had his sons and their wives to help him.

"This would be easier if I had others to help me," Noah said as he wiped the sweat from his wrinkled forehead.

The pair of doves who had happened to make a new nest nearby heard Noah. They knew he was different from the other humans, having spared the tree where they were living as soon as he saw them, and they wanted to help.

"But what can we do?" they wondered.

God spoke to them. "Go and call the other animals - two of each kind - and tell them to come here. They can help Noah build the boat I have asked him to build, and gather seeds and food, then when the boat is done, they can go inside and survive the flood that I will send."

The doves flew out and did as God had told them to do.

One day, to Noah's amazement, the animals began to appear. Many of them did not have pairs of hands, but they could help, and they did. The woodpeckers, squirrels and the beavers helped cut the wood. The monkeys and apes helped to weave the ropes. The elephants, camels, rhinos and buffaloes pulled the logs down and carried them on their backs, while the doves and the other animals gathered seeds and food.

Soon, with everyone working together, the boat was done. It was even larger than Noah thought it would be! He led every animal inside the boat, doing his best to fit everyone in, even the giraffes with their long necks, the thorny devils with their, well, sharp thorns, and the not-so-sweet-smelling polecats. He stuffed the storage room with food and seeds. Now, all that was left to do was to go inside.

Noah took his wife, his sons, and their wives, and they went inside the boat. Afterwards, God closed the door.

Then God gathered the clouds, and it began to rain.

At first, the people were not worried about the rain. After all, it had rained before. They continued with their lives and their evil ways as the drops fell on the ground, on the roofs of their houses, and on the leaves of the trees.

"A little rain never hurt," they thought. "It should stop soon enough."

However, the rain did not stop. The drops kept falling from the sky. Pitter-patter. Pitter-patter.

The puddles turned into ponds then into lakes and seas, combining with the other seas and the rivers, flooding the land. The water went higher and higher, just as high as a person's knees at first, then it went as high as the roofs of houses and the tallest trees.

Noah's boat - and his zoo - began to float. For forty days, as the rain poured, it sailed throughout the Earth, rocked by the waters that soaked every plain, filled every valley, and covered every mountain. Noah and all the animals stayed inside. It wasn't easy taking care of a floating zoo, especially with some animals getting seasick and some making too much noise, but Noah and his family managed, praying every day as they waited for the rain to stop.

One morning, Noah woke up to realize that it was quiet outside, and he looked out the window to find the sun shining.

"The rain has stopped!" he shouted happily.

His family cheered. The animals, too, made even more noise in celebration.

"Now, we just have to wait until the waters dry up," Noah said.

As the water started going down, the boat stopped on top of a mountain. There, Noah and his family and all the animals waited for the waters to dry up. It took many months. Noah's face grew even more wrinkles and his beard grew longer. Some of the animals already had their young. Some of the snakes had shed their skins. It seemed to take forever for the flood to disappear, but finally, one day, Noah saw a spot of land.

"Maybe we can go out of the boat now," he thought.

To make sure, he sent out one of the doves and watched it fly beyond the horizon.

"If it finds even one tree, it will not come back," Noah thought. "And that means my family and the animals can finally go on land."

The dove flew high and low, searching for somewhere to rest its wings, but it only saw water and some mountaintops. By sunset, it returned, and Noah sighed sadly.

"Don't worry, Father," his oldest son comforted him. "Maybe we just have to wait a bit more."

After a week, Noah sent the dove out again. Again, the dove searched for somewhere to land, flying over the waters. There was still so much water, but at least, the dove could also now see some trees with their tallest branches sticking out, one of which was an olive tree. The dove plucked a branch from it and brought it back to Noah.

When Noah saw it, he smiled. "It won't be long before we can go back to land," he thought.

He waited another week, then sent the dove out again. This time, the dove saw much less water and more of the trees. It found a branch that it thought would make a good place for a new home, and there it rested, waiting for the rest of its family.

When the dove did not return to the boat by sunset, Noah rejoiced.

"We can finally go on land!" he shouted joyfully.

Noah opened the window and let all the birds fly out, the female dove and her chicks flying to where the male dove was waiting. Noah and his sons opened the door, and the rest of the animals marched, crawled, and jumped out, heading in every direction.

Noah watched them go with a smile. "I think I will miss them, but I hope they will all find good homes," he said.

Once the boat was empty, Noah gathered his family, and they all prayed to God.

"Thank you for saving us, dear God," he said. "And for making the Earth new."

God blessed Noah and his family.

"Go and have children and grandchildren so that the goodness of humanity may once again spread throughout the land," He said.

Then He painted a curved line in the sky made of glowing colors - a rainbow amid the clouds.

"This is a sign that I will never again send a flood upon creation," God told Noah. "This I promise you and all your descendants and every living creature upon the Earth."

The doves saw the rainbow, and they felt happy. All the other animals also rejoiced, feeling God truly watching over them. Now, they could live in peace.

Noah also felt grateful. He was glad the flood was over and that he would never have to experience one again. Still, he would never forget his floating zoo, not for as long as he lived - up to nine hundred and fifty years old.

The Boy And The King

Once, there was a boy named Joseph who lived in Canaan - the land named after Noah's grandson - with his father, Israel, his ten half brothers, and his younger brother, Benjamin. That's eleven brothers in all! When they were kids, they must have had lots of fun playing together and telling each other stories in the dark as they shared a single tent to sleep in, but as they grew older, they began to drift apart.

One reason for this was that their father, Israel, liked Joseph more than the others. One day, when Joseph was about seventeen, his father gave him a gift - a coat with every color. It was like a piece of the rainbow with stripes of the blue sky, the golden sun, the green grass, the red fruits of the trees, and the purple flowers.

"I didn't know which color you liked best," said Israel. "So I had one made with every color."

"It is the most beautiful coat I have ever seen!" Joseph said as he put it on, then he gave his father a hug. "Thank you, Father. I will take good care of this gift all my life."

When Joseph's brothers heard about the coat, they became even more jealous of him.

"Why did Father have to give Joseph a new coat?" Levi grumbled. "Doesn't he have enough coats already?"

"I'm the one who could use a new coat," Dan said, pointing to the tatters in the one he was wearing.

"And why a coat of so many colors?" Asher asked. "It must have cost three goats at least."

Reuben, the oldest of all of them, frowned. "This is unfair. We are all father's sons, so he should treat us all the same, and yet he dotes on Joseph."

"No wonder Joseph thinks he is so special," Simeon said. "Remember that dream he told us? About the sun and the moon and eleven stars bowing to him? What does that even mean?"

Issachar shook his head. "I think it's time for us to teach Joseph a lesson. Maybe we cannot talk sense into Father, but we can put Joseph in his place and remind him that we are older than he is, so he should respect us."

Zebulun nodded. "But how exactly do we teach Joseph a lesson?"

The brothers found their answer when they were out in the desert one day, herding the goats. As they were sitting in the shade of the trees in the oasis, they saw Joseph coming, his multicolored coat gleaming under the sun.

"This is our chance," Gad said, clenching his fists. "He is alone and far from home. Neither Father nor his dreams can save him now."

Naphtali stretched his arms and nodded. "There is no way he can win against all of us."

Reuben saw what they were planning, and he stood up. "Whoa! Wait a second. Why don't we just talk to Joseph? We will get in trouble if Father finds out that Joseph was hurt."

"Father will not find out," Dan said. "We can leave him in one of the empty wells. No one will ever find him."

Reuben could not believe his ears. He knew his brothers were jealous of Joseph, as he was himself, but there was no need to go too far or for anyone to get hurt.

"If you are going to leave him inside a well anyway, why not just do that?" he suggested. "There is no need for a fight. Just take him and throw him into the well. Like you said, no one will find him there."

As he said this, Reuben already had a plan in mind. Later on, after everyone had left, he would return to rescue

Joseph, sure that his brother would have learned his lesson after spending hours at the bottom of a well, then everything would be fine.

The brothers agreed. "Fine," they said. "But we will take his pretty coat."

As soon as Joseph was near, they grabbed him and dragged him to one of the empty wells, then they seized his coat and threw him inside.

"Brothers!" Joseph called out. "If this is a joke, it isn't funny. Please help me out!"

But his brothers pretended not to hear him, turning their attention back to the goats. None of them seemed to feel bad about what they did, except Reuben, who could not stand to hear Joseph's cries. So he left, determined to return later.

Shortly after, Joseph quieted down. He sat at the bottom of the well and prayed, "Dear God, I don't understand why my brothers did this to me, but I forgive them because I know they are good men at heart, just like Father, and I know that you allowed this to happen for a reason, so I place my trust in you."

At noon, the brothers sat down to have lunch, but before they could start eating, they saw other men approaching - a caravan of merchants. This gave Judah an idea.

"Why leave our brother in the well when we can sell him to these merchants and get some money?" Judah said.

The others thought this was clever and agreed. Judah spoke to the merchants.

"Good sirs, it seems that your camels are loaded with plenty of goods," he said to them. "Why not get someone to carry some of the load off your camels? We happen to have someone strong that you can buy for just twenty pieces of silver."

The merchants looked at their cargo and at each other. "Another travel companion would be nice," they said. "And we can sell him when we reach Egypt."

So Judah and his brothers handed Joseph over to the merchants in exchange for money, and the merchants took him across the desert to Egypt.

Reuben did not know about this, though, so when he returned later in the day to rescue Joseph, he was surprised and devastated to find the well truly empty.

"Where is Joseph?" he asked his brothers.

They told Reuben everything that had happened, and he became even more worried.

"Let us not tell Father," he said. "He will lose his mind and give up everything he has trying to search for Joseph. It is better to tell him that Joseph is gone."

So they tore up his coat, covered it in goat's blood, and showed it to their father. As soon as Israel saw the coat, he knew what tragic fate his beloved son had met, and he began to mourn.

Meanwhile, Joseph had reached Egypt. He was sold as a slave to a man named Potiphar, the captain of the guards of the Pharaoh, the King of Egypt.

Even though Joseph was suddenly far away from his family in a foreign land, made to work harder than he ever had to in his life, he never complained. He did his chores as best as he could. Because of this, Potiphar was impressed with him and made him the man responsible for looking after the whole house and all the other slaves.

Unfortunately, because Joseph spent more time inside the house, he caught the attention of Potiphar's wife. She found him attractive so she tried to get his attention, too, but Joseph wouldn't even look at her.

"I'm sorry," he told her. "You are my master's wife, and my master has been nothing but good to me. I cannot take anything that is his."

This made Potiphar's wife very angry, so that when her husband came home, she lied to him, telling him that Joseph had hurt her. This made Potiphar angry in turn, thinking that Joseph had betrayed his trust, and he had Joseph thrown into prison.

Now behind bars, Joseph felt more alone, but he never lost faith in God. He still never complained and did everything he was told, which made the warden of the prison come to like him. One day, when two new prisoners arrived, the warden entrusted them to Joseph.

"Look after them," he said. "And tell them about all the rules here."

Joseph did just that. He found out that the new prisoners used to work in the palace for the Pharaoh himself - the Pharaoh's butler and his chief baker.

"We'll never get out of here," the butler cried. "Oh, I should never have made the Pharaoh angry."

"This is so unfair," the baker complained. "Why do I have to end up here?"

The two looked even sadder the next day.

"What's wrong?" Joseph asked them.

"I had a strange dream," the butler said. "There was a grapevine with three branches, and I took the fruits, made wine for the Pharaoh, and served him a cup."

Joseph, who still happened to have God's gift of being able to tell the meaning of dreams, gave this some thought and said, "Don't worry. It means that in three days, you will be back in the palace and in Pharaoh's presence again. I hope you will tell him about me."

"What about my dream?" the baker asked. "I dreamed there were three baskets of bread on my head, and birds were eating from the topmost one. Does this mean I will also get out of here soon?"

Joseph sighed. "Yes, you will get out of here in three days, too, but I'm afraid when the guards drag you out, it will be to your grave."

Sure enough, in three days, the butler and the baker were taken out of prison. The butler was brought back to the palace, and the baker was brought to the gallows. Joseph's prophecies had come true, but unfortunately, as soon as the butler got his job back, he forgot about Joseph, and Joseph stayed in prison for two more years.

After two years, the Pharaoh had troubling dreams that he could not stop thinking of and that none of his priests and brightest scholars could make sense of. Only then did the butler remember about Joseph.

"Your Majesty, I know someone who is good at interpreting dreams," he told the Pharaoh. "He was the one who told me I would return to the palace after staying three days in prison, and that is exactly what happened."

The Pharaoh was curious. "Bring this man to me," he ordered.

And so the boy from Canaan was brought before the King of Egypt, and the Pharaoh spoke about his dreams.

"I dreamed that seven healthy cows came out of the river followed by seven cows that were no more than skin and bone, yet the seven sickly cows ate the healthy ones. Then in another dream, I saw seven good ears of corn, but another seven withered ears of corn grew and took their place."

Joseph listened, and he nodded. "Both of these dreams mean the same, Your Majesty. For seven years, Egypt will have good harvests and healthy animals, but for seven years after, there will be a famine, and the plants will not grow, nor will the animals have anything to eat."

The Pharaoh's eyes grew wide. "Are you sure about this?"

Joseph gave another nod. "It isn't me who interprets dreams but God, and it is what God told me."

The Pharaoh believed Joseph, and he gave an order to his officers to store as much food as they could. He also rewarded Joseph, giving him jewelry and making him one of his advisers. With God's grace, the slave boy had become the King's right-hand man.

For the next seven years, Joseph helped the Pharaoh gather and store food, and Egypt ended up having so much that in the seven years of famine that followed, they had more than enough to feed the people, which Joseph helped the Pharaoh sell to people from other countries. Because of this, Egypt prospered even more.

The Baby On The River

Golden sands, cursed mummies in tombs, buried treasure. These are just some of the things the land of Egypt brings to mind. The most amazing symbols of Egypt, though, are the pyramids that are still standing in the desert even after thousands of years. Each pyramid is made of more than two million bricks and stands about as tall as six or seven giraffes standing on top of each other. Of course, they were not easy to make, though. It took plenty of calculations, at least 10,000 workers, and three decades to build a single pyramid. Egypt actually didn't have enough people to build these impressive structures, which is why they bought slaves from different countries, many of which were Hebrews like Joseph.

During Joseph's time, many Hebrews settled in Egypt to escape the famine. They did not mind ending up as slaves as long as they survived. They made their homes in Egypt and had families in Egypt, giving birth to more slaves. At first, the Egyptians did not mind. They even liked the fact that they were getting more workers to build their pyramids, palaces, and temples. However, as the number of the Hebrews continued to increase, the Egyptians became worried.

"They're everywhere like rats," an Egyptian merchant said. "What if they all catch a plague and wipe us out with them?"

"What if they decide to start a war against us?" an Egyptian soldier voiced his concern. "Or worse, join up with our enemies in a war against us?"

An Egyptian priest shook his head. "There are more Hebrews than Egyptians now, and they are strong from working day and night, so they can easily tear down our temples and make us their slaves."

As these whispers on the street grew louder, they reached the ears of the current Pharaoh, and he, too, began to worry.

"Give the Hebrew slaves more work," he ordered. "Then they won't have time to have any foolish ideas."

The Hebrew slaves were given more bricks to carry, more fields to plow, more carts to pull, and yet even though they suffered, their numbers didn't decline.

Watching the throngs of them work under the hot sun, the Pharaoh shook his head. "This will simply not do," he said. "There must be a way to cut the number of Hebrew slaves so that they do not outnumber the Egyptians. This is Egypt, after all."

"What if we get rid of half of the workers?" one of the Pharaoh's advisors suggested. "We can throw them into a pit of snakes or lock them inside one of the pyramids."

Pharaoh snorted. "Who will build the other pyramids if we get rid of the workers?"

"Then maybe we can just get rid of the elderly?" another advisor suggested.

Pharaoh frowned. "Do you really think the elderly can start a war?"

Neither advisor answered.

Pharaoh sighed. "I didn't think so. Instead of the elderly, we should reduce the number of the young and nip the population in the bud. From this day on, I decree that every newborn Hebrew male will be thrown into the river."

Hearing this decree, the Hebrew women wailed. "What will become of our future sons? Is this a sign that God has truly abandoned us?"

One Hebrew woman from the tribe of Levi happened to have just found out that she was carrying her third child, and she clutched her stomach in fear. What if she had another son? What would become of him?

At that moment, she decided not to tell anyone that she was pregnant. "This will be our secret," she told her two older children, Aaron and Miriam. "So be good and make sure you don't breathe a word to anyone."

"We promise we won't," Miriam said. "But what will happen once the baby comes out? Won't everyone know our secret then?"

That was what her mother was worried about, too, but she simply said, "We will think of something when that time comes. In the meantime, we will pray for God's mercy."

The months passed, and the day came for the baby to be born. Just as the Hebrew woman had feared, the baby turned out to be a boy.

"The Egyptians will come for him now," she thought with sorrow in her heart. "But not if I can help it."

She tried her best to hide her son, keeping him inside the house and smothering his cries, but hiding a baby is no easy task.

One day, Aaron came home out of breath from running. "The Egyptian soldiers are coming!" he told his mother. "They are going to take my brother away."

Quickly, his mother took the baby and placed him in the basket she had prepared in case this day would come. It was a basket made of reeds, light enough to float on water, and coated with substances used on the bottom of boats to prevent water from going inside.

She called Miriam and gave her the basket. "Place this on the river where the current is not too strong."

"On the river?" Miriam's eyes grew wide. "But what if he drowns?"

"If the soldiers take him, he will drown anyway," her mother replied. "Take him and let the basket flow with the river while you watch from the bank, then let me know where the river takes him."

"Hurry," Aaron urged from the doorway.

Miriam grabbed the basket and ran out. Her mother fell on her knees and prayed, "Dear God, I place my son in your care. He is yours now. Please watch over him as you watched over my ancestors in their time of need and keep him safe."

Just as her mother had instructed, Miriam placed the basket that had her brother inside on a shallow part of the river. Slowly, the water began to carry it away.

God had heard the Hebrew woman's prayer, and He watched over the basket.

When the current grew stronger and the basket almost tipped over, God asked the turtles to keep it steady. When the basket got caught on some rocks, God asked the birds to give it a lift. When the basket passed through the territory of the hippos and the crocodiles, God told them to leave it alone and keep their big mouths closed.

God also sent a wind to guide the course of the basket, for He knew exactly where He wanted it to end up. The gentle breeze blew the basket around every bend and curve of the winding river while the water rocked it softly to keep the baby inside asleep, and eventually, it reached the palace.

God distracted the guards so they would not see the basket, allowing the river to carry it further inside, all the way to the place where the Pharaoh's daughter took her baths. Then, the basket stopped on the stairs.

As the princess came down to bathe, she saw the basket.

"What is this?" she wondered in surprise.

"Your Highness, be careful," one of her servants said. "We don't know what is inside. What if it is a poisonous snake? Maybe we should call one of the guards to check it first."

Suddenly, though, a babble came from inside the basket, followed by soft coos. Unable to resist, the Pharaoh's daughter opened the basket, and as soon as she saw the baby inside, she gasped. For a moment, the baby just looked at her with his wide eyes, then he started to cry because he did not recognize her. Moved with pity, the princess took the baby in her arms.

"Shh," she whispered to him as she pressed him against her chest and stroked his head. "Everything's alright. You're safe now."

The baby stopped crying. Again, he looked at the princess, and this time, he smiled. At that moment, the princess felt a tug on her heart. She just knew that even though she did not give birth to this baby, he belonged to her. He needed her. He wanted her. And she wanted him.

She planted a kiss on his head. "From this day on, you will be my precious son," she said.

"But, Your Highness, what will your father say?" a servant asked. "Won't he be angry?"

"Why would he be?" the princess replied. "He has always given me everything I want. And I want this baby."

"But he is Hebrew," a servant pointed out. "Just look at the color of his skin and his hair."

"Then I shall just have to get a Hebrew slave to help me take care of him," the princess said.

Miriam, who had been following the basket and watching the whole time while keeping herself hidden, suddenly stepped forward. "Your Highness, I know a Hebrew woman who can help you take care of him," she said.

The servants frowned and scolded Miriam. "What are you doing here, slave girl? How dare you speak to the Pharaoh's daughter."

But the princess told them to be quiet and asked Miriam to come closer.

"Have you been looking after this baby?" she asked.

Miriam nodded.

"Then go and bring me someone who will help me take care of him," she said.

Miriam left to get her mother, telling her everything that had happened. The Hebrew woman could not believe it, but she praised God and rushed to the palace.

"Take care of this child," the princess told her, placing the baby in her arms. "For I will raise him as my own here in the palace. He will be a prince of Egypt and I will make sure he will have everything he needs and wants."

"You are very kind, Your Highness," the baby's mother said. "I will definitely do my best to serve you and take good care of this child. I just have one question. What do you plan on calling him?"

"I will name him Moses," the princess answered. "Because the river brought him to me, and I took him out of the water."

The Hebrew woman smiled. "It is a good name, Your Highness." Then she looked at the baby in her arms and whispered his name. "Moses."

Silently, she added, "May God bless you, my son, for He has kept you safe. He has answered my prayer, and I will ask for nothing more."

Indeed, God blessed Moses, who would become one of God's greatest prophets, a prince to match Pharaoh himself. Just as he was delivered from the river and from the Egyptian soldiers, he would one day deliver the Hebrews from slavery in Egypt.

It's Raining Bread!

H ave you ever been hungry and looked up at the sky, wishing that it would rain doughnuts or chips or biscuits? And what do you think you would do if it really did start raining food? It may seem like magic or wishful thinking but it actually happened to the He-brews thousands of years ago during their exodus, which is a fancy word for a journey made by a large number of people, usually when they are leaving a place for good.

After Moses led the Hebrews out of Egypt, they were over the moon at first. They were no longer strangers in a strange land, and they were no longer slaves. They were free to sleep all day and eat whatever they wanted. At least, that's what they thought, but they were on a journey so they actually still had to carry heavy loads for hours and they had to make their food last.

"I'm tired and hungry," one of them complained. "How is this different from being a slave in Egypt?"

"At least, back in Egypt, I had a bed to sleep on when the night came so I could get a proper rest," said another. "Now, we barely stop to rest, and when we do, we sleep on the ground."

"Back in Egypt, we even had one day of rest a week," one more Hebrew piped in. "But now, I cannot remember the last time we camped or how many days we have been walking. Honestly, I am not sure how much longer I can last."

Moses heard these complaints, but he said nothing. He just left everything to God. After all, it was God, not him, who delivered the Hebrews from Egypt, who performed all those miracles before the Pharaoh and sent those punishments down upon the Egyptians, who parted the sea and made it come together again to drown the Egyptian soldiers who tried to chase after them. Surely, God was leading the Hebrews to a wonderful place, and He would make sure every Hebrew made it there.

Still, when they ran out of water a few days after crossing the Red Sea, even Moses got worried. He thought everything would be fine after they reached a place that had streams, but to his and everyone's dismay, the water was bitter.

"We can't drink this!" a Hebrew man complained after spitting out the water and coughing. "It tastes even more horrible than the worst medicine I've tasted."

A Hebrew woman started to cry. "What will we drink now? The children are already getting sick from not having anything to drink for a day. Without water, they will not last another day, and we will not last much longer either."

"This is a problem," Aaron, Moses' brother, agreed. "We need water in order to survive - clean, fresh water and not whatever is in these streams."

Moses could not ignore this, so he prayed to God. "Dear God, we know You are always watching over us. Please give us water to drink so that we may have the strength to continue on our journey to the place You have promised us."

God replied, "Turn around, and you will see a small tree behind you. Pull it from its roots and throw it into the stream, then the bitter water will turn sweet and everyone will be able to drink and quench their thirst."

Moses did as God had commanded him, and sure enough, the water became good enough to drink. All the Hebrews drank and were refreshed. They refilled their jars, ready to continue their journey.

Seeing the people with their strength and spirit renewed, Moses lifted his eyes to the sky. "Thank you, dear God," he said.

"As long as you follow My words, you are My people," God told Moses. "And I will never let you suffer like I did the Egyptians. I will watch over you and give you strength and heal you of all pain and suffering."

As proof of His faithfulness, God led Moses and the Hebrews to an oasis next, where they found even more water and plenty of trees. It was the perfect place to take a break, so they set up camp and rested.

After a few days, they continued on their journey, and again for a while, all was well. The Hebrews had rested their tired feet and they had plenty of water. The problem was that food continued to dwindle and soon, there was barely any left for anyone to eat. As their empty bellies growled and started to ache, the Hebrews grumbled once more.

"Back in Egypt, we had plenty of meat and bread to eat, enough to last us the whole day," they said. "But now, we are starving. What good is freedom if one is hungry? Have we really been saved or are we just waiting for our bodies to fall apart?"

Again, Moses prayed to God. "Dear God, surely, You can hear the cries of Your people. They are hungry and afraid. You are the only one who can save us, so I ask that You show us Your goodness once more."

God said, "I have heard the cries of the children of Israel, and just as I saved them from slavery, I will save them from hunger. This very evening, they will have meat, and tomorrow morning, they will have bread. This will continue every evening and every morning except for the seventh day. While on the first five days, the people must not store more bread than what they can eat, on the sixth day, they must gather more than enough and put some away so that on the seventh day, they will not go hungry. That day is a day of rest and a day that must be kept holy."

Moses told the Hebrews this, but they were still confused. How exactly was God going to give them meat and bread to eat?

When evening came, they sat down and waited.

"What are we doing, Mother?" a Hebrew child asked.

"Waiting for food," his mother answered. "So be quiet now."

The child, however, did not understand how there would be food. Would it magically appear in his hands or his mouth? He opened his palms, closed his eyes, and waited.

Soon, he heard the wind blowing and the flapping of wings. He opened his eyes, and to his surprise, he saw small birds falling to the ground, one on his hand and another on the top of his head.

The rest of the crowd gasped in amazement and cheered for joy. All this time, they had not seen any wild animals to hunt for food, not even a single bird, but now, God had showered them with a flock of birds, literally placing the creatures on their laps.

A man gathered five of them in his arms and stood up. "Now, we can finally have fresh meat!" he said.

The Hebrews cooked the birds and ate the meat, giving thanks to God for the hearty meal. That night, they slept peacefully with full bellies.

The next day, even before the sun came up, the Hebrews woke up to the feel of something cool and wet against their skin.

"Is it raining, Father?" a child asked as she wiped her skin.

"I don't think so," his father replied, gathering the moisture from the ground on his fingertips. "I think it is just morning dew."

But when the sun came up, the dew evaporated and left behind thin, white, round things on the ground, like snowflakes or coins made of frost.

The child's father picked one up. "What is this?" he wondered out loud. "I have never seen one before."

The child was curious, too, and hungry. Somehow, the round thing just looked good to eat, and she could not help but put it in her mouth.

"Wait!" Her father tried to stop her, but it was too late.

She ate the strange object left by the dew, smiling as she realized it tasted like honey as it melted on her tongue.

"It tastes good!" she exclaimed.

Hearing this, the other people tasted the white flakes, too, and they were also amazed.

"It is like a wafer of bread," one said. "Is this the bread that God promised He would give us?"

"God made it rain bread!" another shouted. "Praise Him for His goodness!"

"It is indeed the bread God promised and sent down from heaven," Moses said. "Now, remember, gather only what you can eat and finish it. It is only on the sixth day that you can gather enough for two days."

The Hebrews gathered the bread, which they called manna, some of them eating it with leftover meat from the night before, others toasting it over a fire. Even though it was thin, it was filling, and everyone was satisfied.

Some, however, disobeyed Moses and set aside more than they could eat, afraid that they would still go hungry. To their dismay, only after a few hours, the manna went bad. It had small worms and a really bad smell!

"This is why I told you not to set aside more than you could eat," Moses scolded them. "Did God not say He would provide food every day? Is that not enough? God has already done so much for you. How long will you keep being stubborn and foolish?"

The people learned their lesson, and they no longer set aside manna, gathering only what they could eat before the manna on the ground melted from the noon sun. Only on the sixth day did they gather plenty and store them in baskets. They were afraid that when they opened their baskets the next day, they would find the manna spoiled, but it wasn't, and they were able to eat well on the seventh day as they rested.

For forty days, as they crossed the wilderness except on every seventh day, God sent the Hebrews quails in the evening and a rain of thin wafers of bread in the morning, and they did not go hungry again.

Who Is Calling Samuel?

Your name is very special. It is something you only share with the people you like and know. This is why when someone calls your name, you can't help but turn your head, and if the person who called you is truly someone you know and like, you stop and smile. But what would you do if you heard a voice call your name and then turned to find nobody there, just like what happened to Samuel?

Samuel's mother was a woman named Hannah, who was married to a man named Elkanah, who also had another wife named Peninnah. Like her husband, she was a kind and prayerful woman, but for many years, God did not give her any children.

"I don't know why Elkanah married someone like you," Peninnah mocked Hannah. "But clearly, I am more worthy of being his wife because I have fulfilled my duty and given him children while you have failed. You are simply a burden and a disgrace to him, and it would be better for us all if you just left."

Hannah knew she had failed, and there were many nights when she would cry herself to sleep. When the time came again for Elkanah to go to the temple in Shiloh to make an offering to the Lord with the whole family, she wanted to stay behind.

"You should just go with Peninnah and your children and leave me alone here at home," Hannah told her husband. "I will only bring you shame if I come along."

However, Elkanah loved Hannah and did not want her to be alone. "I know that Peninnah is mean to you sometimes and that people whisper about you not having children whenever you are out of the house, but try not to be so sad," he said to her as he held her hand. "After all, I am still here. Do I not look after you? Am I not enough to make you happy?"

Hannah loved her husband, too, so even though she did not want to, she went with him to Shiloh. She kept quiet as she watched Elkanah, Peninnah, and their children make their offerings, listening as the other people at the temple wished them well. Those very same people tried to whisper comforting words to her about the fact that she didn't have children, but as soon as she turned her back, she could hear them sighing and feeling sorry for her.

"It's a pity she cannot have children when she is quite beautiful," they said. "But maybe God does not think she will make a good mother."

That night, Hannah barely touched her dinner. She wouldn't have eaten a single bite if Elkanah had not insisted on it, worried for her health. She couldn't sleep a wink either, so while everyone slept, she got up from her bed and went back to the temple. There, she cried her heart out to God.

"God, I know You are all-powerful. You are the Lord of every place and everything in this world. Please show some mercy on this poor handmaid of Yours and give me a son. If You do, I promise You that I will give him back to You so that he may serve You all his life."

She wept, and she prayed at the temple all night, and by early morning, when one of the priests, Eli, saw her, her eyes had grown red. Her lips moved, but not a sound came out, for her voice had already become hoarse.

Eli touched her shoulder. "Woman, are you drunk? If so, you must leave this place at once because this is a holy place."

"No, sir," Hannah replied as she looked at him. "I have never tasted any wine. I have simply been crying."

Eli's eyebrows furrowed. "All night? Do you mean you have not slept?"

Hannah shook her head. "I have been here at the temple pouring out my heart and soul to God all night in the hopes that He will answer my prayer."

Eli could not smell any wine from Hannah so he knew she was not drunk. He could see the deep sadness in her eyes as well, and his heart was moved with pity for her.

"If I feel pity for her, surely, God feels the same," he thought. "And surely, He will not turn her away."

Then Eli said to Hannah, "Stand up and go home. Be at peace, for God in His mercy will surely grant your heart's desire."

Hannah obeyed. As she left the temple, she dried her tears. She felt as if she had shed every tear that she could and laid down all her burdens at God's feet. Now, all that she had left to do was to trust in God's plan for her.

Just as Eli said, Hannah's prayer was answered. She gave birth to a son, which made everyone in the house happy.

Even Peninnah had no desire to grumble. "I am glad that now, you will know the joy of being a mother," she said to Hannah. "It is not all joy and wonder, though, so if you ever feel like you are having a hard time, feel free to ask me for help."

"I always knew you would give me a child," Elkanah told Hannah after planting a kiss on her forehead. "Have you already picked a name for our son?"

"Samuel," Hannah answered. "Because it means God has heard my prayer, and that is exactly what happened."

Elkanah nodded. "Very well. In a few months, we will bring Samuel with us to the temple so that God's blessing may be upon him."

But Hannah shook her head. "I am not going to the temple in Shiloh this year or anytime soon. I will only go when Samuel is old enough because when I bring him to the temple, I will no longer bring him home. Rather, I will leave him there at the temple to serve the Lord just as I promised the Lord."

Elkanah was surprised to hear this, but he understood. "Do whatever you think is best and pleasing to the Lord," he told her.

Hannah took care of Samuel for the next few years, and when he was old enough to clothe and feed himself, Hannah brought him to the temple in Shiloh along with plenty of gifts, which she gave to Eli.

He did not recognize her at once, so she had to remind him. "I was the woman you found crying here at the temple," Hannah said.

Eli took a good look at Hannah. "That was you? You definitely look better now."

"You told me that God would grant my heart's desire, and He did," Hannah said. "He gave me a son, and now, I am here to give my son back to Him."

Eli looked at the boy and then at Hannah. "Are you saying you want your only son to stay here at the temple to serve the Lord? Are you sure about this?"

Hannah nodded. "There is no one more powerful than God. Indeed, who else can give life or give barren women sons? I have made Him a promise. How can I not be true to it?"

Eli was impressed with Hannah's words, so he took Samuel's hand. "Very well," he said. "From now on, your son will be a child of this temple, and both God and I will look after him."

God was pleased with Hannah and gave her more children. As for Samuel, he stayed at the temple from that day forward, helping the priests with the offerings during the day and praying at night before going to sleep, and God was pleased with him as well.

A few years later, after Samuel had just gone to sleep, he suddenly heard a voice calling him.

"Samuel," the voice whispered.

At once, Samuel sat up. "I'm here," he said as he rubbed the sleep from his eyes.

But when he opened his eyes, he saw no one around. The room was completely dark and not a sound could be heard.

"Maybe I was dreaming," Samuel thought.

Still, he lit a candle and stayed awake. After a few moments, he heard the voice again.

"Samuel," it called to him.

Samuel heard the voice clearly, and he thought it must be Eli calling him as the old priest usually did, so he ran to Eli's room.

"I'm here," he said. "Is there anything I can do for you, sir?"

Eli woke up, surprised. "What do you mean, boy?" he asked. "I did not call for you. Go back to bed."

Samuel was puzzled, but he went back to his bed. No sooner had he rested his head on the pillow did he hear the voice calling his name again.

"Samuel."

Samuel ran to Eli's room. "You called me, so I am here," he said.

Eli looked at him with a frown. "My boy, I did not call your name. Go back to sleep, and let me sleep as well."

Samuel obeyed, but he was still very much confused. He knew what he had heard. Who was calling him? And why?

When the voice called him again, he returned to Eli's room.

"I am sure you called me," Samuel said. "So here I am."

However, Eli knew that it was not he who called Samuel. If Samuel could really hear someone calling him, Eli had only one guess who it could be.

"The next time you hear the voice, stay in your room and say, 'Speak, Lord, for your servant is listening,'" Eli told Samuel.

Samuel returned to his room. Again, the voice called his name, and this time, Samuel answered as Eli had told him to.

"I am here, Lord. Speak, for your servant is listening."

It was indeed God who was calling Samuel, and that night, God spoke to Samuel for the first time. It would mark the beginning of his life as one of God's prophets, the voice and hand of God who would guide Israel for many years.

In The Belly Of A Whale

What can get about as big as an airplane, can make sounds louder than the chimes of the Big Ben and can eat as much food as five thousand tubs of ice cream a day? A whale, of course. Indeed, the belly of a whale is so huge that it can fit so much food. And you know what else can fit inside its stomach? As many as fifteen grown men. Isn't it a good thing that whales do not eat people? Still, there was one man who once found himself in this giant sea creature's stomach - a prophet named Jonah.

Jonah's journey as a prophet started the same way Samuel's did - he heard a voice calling him in the middle of the night.

"Open your eyes, Jonah."

Jonah did open his eyes but he did not see anyone standing by his bed, so he scratched his head. "Who is it?"

"It is I, your God," the voice answered. "And I have a task for you. Go to the city of Nineveh where the people have done many things to make me angry. Tell them that they must change their ways, or else they will know just how angry they have made Me."

Jonah was someone who grew up believing in God, so he knew it was God who was speaking to him. He also remembered all the stories he had been told about the past prophets - both about the miracles they performed and the hardships they endured. He wasn't sure if that was the kind of life he wanted or a job that he could do.

"Are you sure you're talking to the right guy?" he asked. "I'm sorry, but I don't think I'd make a good prophet. I can't even talk in front of a large group of people without my hands shaking. If I stand before a king, my legs might just wither under me."

God, however, had chosen him and kept calling his name in the middle of the night. Finally, Jonah grew tired.

"I will run away," he thought. "I will go far away from him so that God will know that I have absolutely no desire to become His prophet and hopefully leave me alone."

Jonah left town and made his way to the city of Joppa. There, he boarded a ship headed to Tarshish in the opposite direction of Nineveh.

"Going to big old Tarshish, young man?" the captain of the ship asked Jonah after he arrived on deck. "May I ask what awaits you there? Long-lost family? Fortune? A woman, maybe?"

"It is not so much that I want to find something there as I want to leave this place," Jonah replied.

The captain tilted his head. "Oh, I see. Escaping from something, are we? Or is it someone?"

"Someone persistent," Jonah replied. "But too powerful for me to get rid of."

The captain shrugged. "In that case, what makes you think you can escape?"

Jonah frowned. "Just take me to Tarshish," he said. "I will worry about the rest."

The captain gave him a salute. "Aye." Then he looked at the sky. "Don't worry. We have good weather and strong winds. We will surely reach Tarshish before you know it."

Little did the captain and Jonah know that God was listening to their conversation.

"Jonah thinks he can ignore and escape me?" God laughed. "Well, I suppose he'll have to learn the hard way that he can't."

Shortly after the ship had started sailing out to sea, God stirred the clouds, the wind, and the waters, brewing a storm. As it tossed the ship from side to side, the people aboard held on to whatever they could to keep themselves from being thrown off, crying out in fear.

"The ship will sink!" a man wailed. "It will be in pieces long before it reaches Tarshish, and all of us will be lost to the sea."

"But why is this happening?" another whined. "The weather was perfect, and the sea was calm when we left the port of Joppa. Now, it almost seems as if the sea is angry with us."

The captain, too, was confused, and he said, "Maybe it is the gods who are angry with us."

"But why?" the passengers asked. "What did we do wrong?"

The captain didn't answer, looking at the passengers one by one to see who was the likely culprit. As his gaze landed on a sleeping Jonah, he frowned.

"How can someone sleep in a situation like this?" he wondered. Then he walked over to Jonah, nearly slipping on the way. "Wake up, young man! How can you be peacefully dreaming when the sea is throwing a fit?"

Jonah shook off the captain's arm and groaned. "I said I didn't want to be a prophet, didn't I?"

The captain's eyebrows arched. A prophet? Then he understood. He shook Jonah harder until finally, Jonah opened his eyes.

"What is happening?" he asked.

"Look around you," the captain told him. "Everyone is scared of the storm and desperately praying to their god. How about you do the same?"

Jonah shook his head. "I cannot call on him. I will not."

Again, the captain frowned. "You've made your god angry, haven't you?"

Then he turned to the other passengers. "This man refuses to call upon his god. I think it is he who has done something wrong. Does anyone else feel the same way?"

The other passengers nodded their heads.

"We have all been shaking in fear," one of them said. "Yet this man has been sleeping and does not seem to care. Maybe it is he who has doomed us all."

Several others murmured in agreement.

The captain looked at Jonah. "Tell me, who are you, and which people do you belong to? Who is your god?"

"I am but a Hebrew named Jonah," Jonah answered. "My god is the God of all, of everything above the sea, under the sea, and on land."

"And yet you do not want to ask him for his mercy and for his help," the captain said. "Which means you have committed a grave sin against him."

"We must throw him out," the other passengers said. "Let us throw him off the ship, then maybe his god will leave us alone."

The captain said nothing, trying to think of a way to save all of his passengers, but as the winds and the waves grew stronger, he knew there was a chance the ship would not make it through the voyage. He should at least try to save most of his passengers.

"I'm sorry," he told Jonah. "But as captain, I must make sure my ship remains in one piece and as many of my passengers as possible survive."

"I understand," Jonah said. "Do what you must."

And so Jonah was tossed overboard, creating a big splash as he hit the water. Shortly after, the wind and the sea stopped throwing a fit, like children who had been given the treat they wanted.

The captain of the ship was amazed. "His god is truly a great and powerful god to create a storm in the blink of an eye and then make it go away," he said. "I am sure he can save Jonah if he wants. If not, there is nothing Jonah or anyone can do."

With each passing second, Jonah continued to sink into the depths of the sea, the strong current just kept pulling him under in spite of his efforts to swim to the surface. Soon, his legs went numb, and it was getting hard for him to breathe, too.

"Is this what I get for trying to escape from God?" he wondered. "I have been so foolish thinking that I could. I should have known that God has a plan and a means to accomplish everything."

As his strength left him and his mind started to slip away, Jonah's life flashed before his eyes. He thought of all the things he had done and all the things he still wanted to do. Maybe if he could turn back time, he would obey God and go to Nineveh. At least, he would try talking to the people there. It was too late now, though, or so Jonah thought.

A few miles away, God was already speaking to Jonah's savior - the biggest creature in the ocean.

"Jonah may be foolish, but I know that his heart is still good," He said to the whale. "I may be able to make use of him yet, so go and save him."

The whale turned around and swam towards Jonah, swallowing him whole.

When Jonah opened his eyes, he found himself inside what seemed like a dark, wet cave.

"Is this the afterlife?" he wondered, but then he heard a rumbling, and he felt the floor move beneath his feet, making him frown. "What kind of cave moves and makes noise?"

He tried to stand up, but he couldn't because the floor was too slippery. The walls were slimy, too, plastered in seaweed.

"Where am I?"

"Jonah, son of Amittai," God's voice rumbled through the air. "You are in the belly of a whale. I saved you because I know you will make a good prophet, and I am still willing to give you that chance."

Jonah sighed. "You really are persistent, aren't you?"

"Didn't you say if you could have another chance, you'd go to Nineveh and try spreading My word?"

Jonah remembered that he did. "Do you really think I will make a good prophet?" he asked.

"I know it," God said. "Just set aside your fears and trust in Me."

Jonah nodded. "Very well, I will go to Nineveh just as You asked. I am sorry I did not do so before. I am ashamed of how I acted, actually. From now on, I will try to be better."

Jonah prayed for three days and nights. During this time, God led the whale to Nineveh, and when the whale had arrived there, God commanded it to spit Jonah out.

The water around Jonah began to rise. Soon, he was floating and swirling, and he felt afraid, so he tried to hang on to a piece of seaweed.

"Let go," God whispered to him. "Trust me."

Jonah let go of the seaweed he was holding on to, and as soon as he did, a powerful current washed him away. He did not know where he was being taken, but he closed his eyes and placed his trust in God. By the time he opened them, he was already on land, the sand beneath him and the sun shining on his face.

He stood up and turned around, seeing a fountain of water on the horizon. Then he heard a bellow.

"That must be the whale that swallowed me," he thought.

He could not believe that he had just spent three days in the belly of a whale. Other people probably wouldn't believe it, too, if he told them. Then again, he had more important things to say. He was a prophet now, after all.

Jonah entered the city of Nineveh, and just as God had told him, he told the people to abandon their greed and their wickedness. He did not expect them to listen, but they did. Even the king began to cry and beg God for forgiveness, promising to lead his people in living a better life. When God saw this, He decided not to destroy Nineveh, but rather give it another chance just as he had given his newest prophet, Jonah.

God's Chosen One

In the court of Heaven, the angels gathered, waiting for their missions from God.

"I can't wait to fly down to Earth and help someone," said one of the helper angels. "Maybe I can save someone who's drowning or help a farmer's crops grow."

"I'm sure it will be thrilling to help a lost child find his way home," one of the guide angels said. "Or simply help someone who's lost hope find his way again."

"Not as thrilling as protecting a traveler from robbers," replied a guardian angel. "Or a shepherd from a pack of hungry wolves or even bears."

"I just want to give someone God's medicine and make them better," a healer angel said. "Then there will be one less person suffering."

The messenger angel had something to say, too. "I hope I'll be asked to deliver good news. I don't want to be one of those angels who warns about punishment or danger."

"It's all up to God, though," said another messenger angel. "Whatever message God gives us, it is exactly what a person needs to hear, and we will deliver it no matter what."

"We are all here to serve God, after all," the harpist in the choir of angels said. "Everything is for His honor and glory."

Suddenly, they heard a strong wind sweeping through the pillars of golden clouds. They all stopped speaking, knelt down, and bowed their heads.

"Gabriel," God called.

The leader of the messenger angels stood up and stepped forward.

The other messenger angels began to whisper. "God only sends Gabriel to really important people or to deliver really important news. What can it be this time?"

"I am sending you to relay important good news to two people this time," God told Gabriel. "I've been watching over the first for a long time, and I know he has been faithful. As for the second, I have chosen her for a special role long before she was born. Now, it is time for her to know what her role is in the greatest story that is yet to be told."

Gabriel bowed his head. "Always and forever, I am at your service, my Creator."

God gave Gabriel two scrolls which disappeared as soon as the angel had finished reading them. Then he walked to the edge of the clouds, opened his large wings, and flew off. The other angels looked down, watching him. They were all curious to know who Gabriel was visiting.

They watched excitedly as Gabriel visited an old priest named Zacharias in the temple, letting him know that even though he and his wife, Elisabeth, were already very old, they would be blessed with their first child, a son to pave the way for God's own son.

After that, the angels had to wait a while, and finally, when Elisabeth was six months pregnant, Gabriel went on his second mission, flying to the city of Nazareth in Galilee.

The angels were even more excited now. Who could this person be that God said He had chosen for a special role? They looked at all the women who were living in Nazareth. They saw a bedridden woman who, before getting very sick, weaved the most beautiful tapestries. They saw a widow who was trying to manage the vineyard her husband left her as best as she could. There was also an old woman who was skilled at making medicine and a young woman who had recently narrowly survived a fire. Could any of these women be the one Gabriel was going to visit?

Then they saw a few women gathered around a well, the youngest of whom was a woman named Mary. She wore only plain clothes, but it was clear that she was beautiful, though what the angels saw even more clearly was her pure heart.

"Please allow me to help you with that," she said to an older woman, pulling on the rope to get a pail of water out of the well.

"Thank you, Mary," the older woman answered, stepping aside. "You really are very kind."

Mary grabbed the pail of water, grunting at its weight. "It's heavier than it looks. I'm not sure you will be able to carry it home. I can do that for you if you want. After all, you don't live far from here."

The old woman raised her eyebrows. "Are you sure? How about your own pail? Didn't you come to the well because you needed water, too?"

"I can get mine later," Mary said. "Let us get you water first."

The old woman nodded. "If you insist."

"I do."

Mary lifted the pail and started walking, doing so slowly because the pail was full, and she wanted to spill as little water as possible. It was heavy especially for her thin arms, but she did not complain or even frown.

"Really, Mary, you are too kind," the old woman told her. "That carpenter, Joseph, is lucky that you were the one chosen for his wife. Aren't the two of you having your wedding soon?"

"Yes," Mary answered. "And I am the lucky one because Joseph is hard-working, kind, and most especially, God-fearing."

"Just like you," the old woman said. "I can see the two of you going together to the temple often. I am sure you will make a fine couple and be blessed with many children."

"I will be happy with any number of children God chooses to bless me with," Mary said. "Even if He gives me just one, I will rejoice because being a mother is the greatest blessing and honor."

"It is a very challenging role, too," the old woman remarked. "But I am sure that you will make an amazing mother."

Finally, they reached the old woman's house. Mary brought the pail of water inside the kitchen and put it down.

"Thank you, child," the old woman told her.

Mary smiled. "It is God we must thank for giving us water and the strength to go about our daily lives. It is thanks to Him that I can do all I can."

The old woman patted Mary's shoulder. "May God bless you even more then."

Mary returned to the well and drew water for herself, then she headed home. By then, the sun was already beginning to set, and when she got home, she found the orange streaks of dying sunlight streaming in through the window. She decided to hurry to prepare dinner before the sun disappeared completely, grabbing her jar of flour, but she nearly dropped it when she heard a voice.

"Greetings," the voice said.

At first, Mary felt fear, thinking that some stranger had been waiting inside her house, but when she turned her head, she saw the angel sent by God, and she was able to breathe. She was still nervous, though, not sure what she should say. Should she offer the angel some food and a room for the night? Should she prostrate herself before him?

"Don't worry, Mary," the angel told her, sensing her anxiety. "You are God's chosen one, the one he has picked to play a special role in the greatest story to be known to man. As of this moment, you have become the mother of the Son of God, of a future king just like your ancestor, David, but unlike David or any other king, his rule will never come to an end."

Mary felt confused as she touched her belly. "Joseph and I are not yet married, but you are saying that right now, there is a baby in my womb?"

"Yes, because God has given you His greatest blessing. Even now, life has begun inside your womb, and when your son is born, he will be known as the Son of God Most High, the God who can do all things. Why, even your cousin, Elisabeth, is expecting a child now because of God's grace. This, too, was a miracle and a blessing given by God."

Mary nodded, fell to her knees, and bowed her head. "My whole life is in God's hands. He created me and made me who I am today, so whatever role He wishes me to play, whatever He wishes me to do, let it be so."

When she looked up again, the angel was gone. He had disappeared without a sound, just like the sunlight that was now fading.

The next day, Mary left on a journey to visit her cousin, Elisabeth, not because she wanted to see if what the angel said was true - she knew it was - but because she wanted to offer her sincere congratulations and help out.

Mary and Elisabeth had not seen each other in years, and they had not written to each other either, and yet when Elisabeth saw Mary, God's grace came upon her, and she just knew that Mary had also received a great blessing from God.

"Mary!" Elisabeth ran to greet her, giving her a hug. "Praise be to God who made us both mothers and who chose you to be the mother of His Son. May His goodness and mercy be remembered forever."

Mary stayed in Elisabeth and Zacharias' house for three months, leaving just shortly before Elisabeth gave birth to John, the prophet who would prepare everyone for the coming of Jesus.

The Night The Angels Sang

On your birthday, you get a cake with candles, presents, and plenty of smiles and well wishes. This is because the people who love you remember how happy they were the day you were born. Indeed, the birth of a baby can bring so much joy to so many people, and there was one that made even the angels celebrate.

After the angels in Heaven heard Gabriel's message to Mary, they all became excited.

"God's Son will be born soon!" they shouted. "We must get ready!"

"We will help Mary and Joseph as much as we can," the helper angels said. "And maybe some can stay here and build a new palace for God's Son."

"We will keep Mary, Joseph, and the baby safe," the guardian angels promised.

"We will guide those who want to visit the baby and pay their respects after he is born," a group of guide angels said. "He is going to be a king after all, like David, his ancestor."

"He will be the best king ever!" some other angels praised.

"Did you hear that?" The trumpeter spoke to the other members of the choir of angels. "There is going to be a big celebration soon, so let us rehearse and give our best performance yet."

"Absolutely!" the others replied.

"Can I be the one to sing the solo part this time?" a cherubim asked. "I haven't had the chance to sing yet."

The other angels in the choir, however, looked at each other and shook their heads. "Maybe some other time. This is a really important performance. The starring role should go to the one with the most experience so we can be sure everything goes perfectly. We don't want to disappoint God, do we?"

The cherubim felt sad, but she didn't want to give up. She was determined to practice and to help as much as she could.

As it so happened, at that time, Joseph was in need of a bit of cheering up. He had just found out that Mary was pregnant days before their wedding, and he knew the baby was not his.

"I can't believe Mary would break my trust," he thought. "I cannot marry a woman who is already carrying the child of another man, nor can I be a father to a child that is not mine. Still, I cannot just call off my wedding to Mary. People will gossip about her or, worse, throw rocks at her. I still love her, so I cannot stand the idea of her getting hurt."

As Joseph was wondering what he should do, the cherubim sang to him, hoping that her sweet voice would lighten Joseph's spirits. The song was so beautiful that it put Joseph to sleep.

As Joseph slept, another angel appeared in his dream with a message. "Don't worry, Joseph. You can wed Mary because she has been faithful to you. The child she is carrying is the Son of God, who will be called Jesus, the Emmanuel - God who is with His people. Just as Mary has been chosen to be the child's mother, you have been chosen to help raise it as his father."

When Joseph woke up, he finally understood everything. His mind was clear, and his heart felt light, and he no longer had any doubts or worries about taking Mary as his wife. They had their wedding as planned and looked forward to the birth of their child. They were hoping to have the child in their home in Nazareth, but those plans were about to change.

One day, as Joseph was finishing up his masterpiece - a crib for the baby Jesus - one of his friends started shouting, "Joseph! Joseph! There's important news!"

"What news?" Joseph wondered out loud.

"The governor has just declared a census because the Emperor wants more taxes," Joseph's friend said. "That means that we all have to return to our hometowns, have our names listed there, and pay tax there."

Joseph's eyebrows furrowed. "But that means I have to go to Bethlehem, where I was born."

"Yes," his friend replied. "And you have to take Mary with you."

Joseph frowned. "But Bethlehem is very far away, and Mary will give birth to our child soon."

The other man placed a hand on Joseph's shoulder. "I'm sorry, my friend, but I am neither the Emperor nor the governor, and they are the ones who say what we must do. We have only to follow."

Joseph had no choice but to take Mary, leave their home and the baby's crib behind, and make the long, hard journey to Bethlehem.

It was indeed a difficult journey, with hardly any shade from the hot sun during the day and only the hard ground to sleep on at night. The wind was getting colder each day, too, with winter approaching.

"It seems like winter this year is going to be the coldest ever," Joseph thought. "I hope that Mary and I will be able to find a warm place where we can stay when we reach Bethlehem."

In spite of all the difficulties, Mary never complained. Even though it must have been so hard sitting on the back of a donkey for hours when her stomach was already so round and heavy, she kept going and kept smiling. Joseph tried to be strong for her as well, even though it pained him to know she must be suffering. If only he could carry her burden, he would.

It was Mary's role, though, to carry her child and the donkey's to carry them both. Sometimes, it was the donkey that wanted to complain, though it could not, so instead, it would just give up and come to a complete stop. Once, it even threw a fit, thinking its hooves could not keep going on the long, rocky road.

During that time, the cherubim sang a song to calm it down, and indeed, it did. After that, each time the donkey was on the verge of another fit, the cherubim started singing, and so the donkey kept going, one worn down hoof in front of the other.

After weeks that felt like years, Mary and Joseph arrived in Bethlehem. It was evening when they entered the city, and to their surprise, there were so many people around.

"I did not expect there to be this many people," Joseph said. "But I suppose a lot of people have come home for the census. I hope there is still an available room at the inn."

However, there was none. Joseph and Mary had taken too long in their journey so every room had already been taken.

"Where will we stay now?" Joseph wondered. "I have to find a place quickly because Mary and the donkey are already exhausted, and it has already grown very cold. Soon, it will be freezing out here."

Just as he said this, Mary's stomach started to hurt. "I think I will have the child soon," she told Joseph.

Joseph hurried to find a room where Mary could safely give birth. He went to every house, hoping that they could let him rent a room.

"Please let us rent one of your rooms," he begged. "You may not know me, but my parents were born here in Bethlehem. Also, my wife is going to give birth any second."

Unfortunately, there was just no room to be found.

"We're sorry," a couple said as they met Joseph at the door to their home. "But we are already staying in one room with our four children just so two other families can stay in our house."

Joseph kept looking. "I'm sorry," he told Mary. "But I promise I will find a place for us."

When they had reached the edge of the city, Joseph thought of going to the next even though it was already late, but Mary put a hand on his arm.

"I don't think I can last much longer," she told him. "Our baby is about to come out."

The helper angels knew about the problem at hand, and they quickly got to work. They didn't have enough time to make a house, but they were at least able to make a stable with a manger and fill it with hay.

Joseph saw it and looked inside, finding only hay. He knew that hay was used to make beds for animals, not people and especially not a woman about to give birth, but it was still better than the cold, hard ground. He knew, too, that the stable was a shelter for animals, but it was better than none. It would still be freezing, but at least they would not be completely exposed to the cold winds.

Joseph led the donkey and Mary to the stable and went inside. There, Mary gave birth to Jesus. As she rested, Joseph wrapped the baby up to keep him as warm as possible, and let him sleep inside the manger, the place usually filled with oats and grains for the horses to eat, because there was no crib and nowhere else to put him.

Meanwhile, the guide angels put up the brightest star in the heavens just above the stable to let the world know that the Son of God had been born, while the messenger angels appeared to the shepherds in the nearby meadow, who were struggling to stay awake while they watched over their grazing sheep. One shepherd was about to fall asleep, in fact, so when he saw the angels, he was so startled that he fell off the rock he was sitting on. Even then, he pinched himself to make sure he wasn't already dreaming.

"Don't be afraid," the messenger angels said. "We have good news, the happiest news, in fact. Tonight, a savior has been born. You will find him sleeping in a manger in a stable in Bethlehem."

Afterwards, the choir of angels took over, the musicians ready with their shiny instruments. The festive music began to play, but no one was singing.

The cherubim, who was watching from afar, was confused. Why wasn't anyone singing?

Just then, some members of the choir of angels called her. "Come and sing with us!"

The cherubim was surprised. "Me? But I thought you said I shouldn't sing."

"We know you have been practicing and that you helped Mary and Joseph get to Bethlehem," they said. "It is only right that you sing tonight."

The cherubim did not need any more convincing. She took her place in the middle of the choir and raised her voice. Her sweet song was heard far and wide, by the sleeping baby Jesus and by every animal on Earth who also joined in the celebration. During the chorus, the other angels sang along, too.

"May God Most High receive all glory on Earth, and may every good heart find peace on this blessed night and forever."

It was truly their most dazzling performance!

Afterwards, the choir of angels returned to Heaven, all except the cherubim, who decided to stay by Jesus' side to sing him lullabies.

The shepherds came with their sheep to worship the newborn Savior. Some animals from the city came as well to pay homage to the Son of God.

When Mary saw them, her exhaustion vanished, and she smiled at all the visitors as she cradled Jesus in her arms. Joseph stood by her side proudly. He had already forgotten about how cold and small the stable was. At that moment, he was the richest, happiest man.

It was a perfect night, a night that would be remembered and celebrated and sung about for ages to come and just the beginning of the greatest story ever told.

Fishers Of Men

After you are born, your parents become your first friends, playing with you and teaching you a lot of things. Then as you grow up, you go outside the house into the world, and you meet other kids that become your new playmates, your new friends. You go to school, and you get even more friends, some of whom become your friends for a very long time to come. Maybe one of them becomes your best friend for life. Even when you're older, you can still make new friends to make and share memories with, just like Jesus did. He got his closest friends when he was already thirty years old. He had twelve of them, in fact.

After Jesus was baptized by his cousin, John, in the Jordan River, he spent more than a month by himself in the desert. When he returned, he was met with sad news - John had been thrown into prison. As much as he wanted to visit his cousin, he knew that it was dangerous, so instead, he left Nazareth and traveled towards the Sea of Galilee, which is actually a large lake, staying at one of the towns around it called Capernaum. Traveling, however, made Jesus feel more alone.

"John is not only my cousin but my closest friend right now," he thought. "If anything happens to him, I won't have any more friends, and I need someone to help me with the work my Father in Heaven has given me."

The next morning, as Jesus was walking along the shore of the Sea of Galilee, he saw two fishermen - Simon and his brother, Andrew - who had their fishing nets over their shoulders and were about to board their small boat.

"Sons of Jonah, how would you like to try catching men instead?" Jesus asked them.

Andrew was surprised. "How does this man know who we are?" he wondered. "I don't think we've met him before. I don't even think he's from around here."

"What do you mean catch men?" Simon asked, thinking it was some kind of riddle.

"Exactly what I said," Jesus answered. "If you follow me, I will make you fishers of men instead of fishermen. You will capture the hearts of men and open them to the ways of God. You will cast words and deeds instead of nets, and you will bring good people into the Kingdom of God."

Andrew became even more confused. "Who is this man?" he asked his older brother. "Is he the spirit of the prophet from long ago, Elijah? Or is he the new prophet, John the Baptist?"

Simon's eyes, however, had been opened by the grace of God, and he went up to Jesus and said, "You are the Son of God, aren't you?"

Then Simon knelt before him, bowing his head, while Andrew stared in awe.

Jesus placed his hand on top of Simon's head. "Simon, the only one who could have told you about this is my Father, and if He told you, then he must trust you to be my friend. From now on, you will be my friend and my rock, so I will call you Peter. With you, I will build my kingdom and my church that will triumph over all evil."

Then he pulled Peter to his feet.

"I will go wherever you go, Lord," Peter said.

Jesus then looked at Andrew. "Would you like to come and be my friend as well?"

Andrew threw aside his net, left the boat, and stood before Jesus. "Being a fisher of men does not sound so bad," he said. "Nor does being a friend of the Son of God."

Jesus put his finger to his lips. "That is our secret, though, so you must promise not to tell anyone."

The brothers nodded. They followed Jesus as he continued to walk along the shore, and soon, they saw another pair of brothers - John and James - who were on a boat with their father, Zebedee. It seemed as if they had just finished fishing, their nets heavy with their catch.

James waved to Peter. "Where are you going? Aren't you going fishing? Don't worry. There are plenty left to catch."

"Who is that man with you?" John asked.

Jesus stepped forward. "James and John, come with me and become fishers of men, then I will call you my friends."

The sons of Zebedee were also confused at first, but they knew Peter and Andrew, and they knew those two would not just follow anyone.

John turned to Zebedee. "I'm sorry, Father, but I am being called, so I will go."

James, too, decided to leave his father behind. "I want to see if I can be something more than a fisherman," he said.

Zebedee nodded. "Then go, and may God watch over you both."

A few days later, as Jesus was passing through the next city with his new friends, he saw a man collecting taxes. At that time, tax collectors were usually seen as greedy men, getting money from the poor and keeping some for themselves. However, Jesus saw that this tax collector's heart was pure, so he approached him.

"If you're going to pay your taxes, tell me your name so I can find it on my list," the tax collector said.

"You may not know my name, but I know yours," Jesus said. "Matthew, I know you are a good man. How would you like to be a fisher of men instead of being someone who collects money from them? Wouldn't you rather collect followers of the word of God? If you do, come with me and be my friend."

Matthew left his desk and joined Jesus and his friends.

The Pharisees, who were strict followers of the law of God, learned about what happened and frowned.

"Why is someone like you who preaches the word of God friends with a tax collector?" a Pharisee asked Jesus. "Don't you know they are sinful?"

"If you are healthy, do you need a doctor?" Jesus asked in return. "Only the sick do. I have come to heal the sick, to open the hearts of those who have sinned so they can change their ways."

Jesus also invited another fisherman, Philip, who happened to come from the same hometown as Peter and Andrew, to be his friend. Philip accepted the invitation, but his friend, Nathanael, disapproved.

"Are you sure he is the promised Savior?" Nathanael scoffed as he stood under a fig tree. "Isn't he a Nazarene? Nazarenes are not to be trusted."

Philip grabbed his hand. "Come and meet him for yourself."

As soon as Nathanael came close to Jesus, Jesus pointed him out. "Now, there is a true Israelite."

Nathanael was puzzled by Jesus' words. "You know me?"

"You are Nathanael, right?" Jesus said. "And you were standing under a fig tree until just a few minutes ago when Philip came to get you."

Nathanael was amazed and knelt before Jesus, bowing his head. "I'm sorry I doubted you. I believe now that you are the promised Savior, the Son of God, the true king of Israel."

"Because I said I saw you under a fig tree?" Jesus laughed. "I promise you that you will see much greater things."

Nathanael believed this, and he said goodbye to his friend, knowing that Philip had made the right decision to follow Jesus.

Jesus called six other men to be his friends - Bartholomew, Thomas, another James who was the son of Alphaeus, another Simon who was from Canaan, Judas Thaddaeus, and Judas Iscariot - a total of twelve friends who would be Jesus' travel companions and closest friends, helping him heal the sick, drive out demons and most importantly, preach the word of God.

"Go like shepherds and help bring back the lost sheep of Israel," Jesus told them. "Go like fishermen into the dangerous sea and bring back an overflowing catch. I have given you God's blessing. Give it to whomever you find worthy, so that together, we can establish the kingdom of my Father."

Seeds In The Wind

As Jesus became popular, people started calling him different things. Some called him a prophet, just like Moses, Elijah, and Jeremiah. Some looked at him as a leader, the king that Israel needed. To the sick, he was a doctor. To the lost, he was a shepherd. More than anything, though, he was a teacher, 'rabbi' in Jewish, and like the best teachers, he was good at telling stories to make his listeners understand and remember his lessons, just like his stories about seeds.

One of the stories Jesus told was about a gardener. This gardener was an expert on seeds, knowing just when and where to plant them, which was why he had a beautiful garden, but one day, as he looked at a bunch of seeds in his hand, he decided to try something else.

"What if I just throw these seeds out in the open?" he wondered. I'll let the wind decide where they'll fall and see how they do."

The seeds actually heard this, and they became excited. "We're going on a journey!" they shouted as they jumped for joy.

Thankfully, they already had their backpacks with them, filled with almost everything they needed for the journey. "All we need now is soil to sleep in and sunlight to cook our food."

"Since we're on our own, why don't we have a contest?" one of the seeds said. "Whoever manages to set up camp and survive for a week wins."

The others liked this idea. "Let's go!"

After the gardener scattered the seeds, the wind carried them away.

"We're flying!" they shouted happily as the wind carried them over the flowers in the garden and high above the trees. The wind even took them for a spin in the clouds so that for a moment, they became covered in the soft, white fluff, which left their coats moist after the wind blew them away. Then the wind carried them over the river, so close to the water's surface that they could see their reflections, and over the meadow where they waved at the other plants.

Afterwards, the wind split in four different directions, scattering the seeds into four groups.

"See you later!" one group shouted. "And may the best seeds win!"

For a while, the wind kept blowing, then it suddenly stopped. As the seeds began to fall, they opened their parachutes and braced for impact. Soon, they hit the ground.

The first group of seeds found themselves on a wasteland. As much as they tried to dig into it to set up camp underground, they could not. The ground was simply too hard.

"We have to go somewhere else," they thought, but as they were on the move, they were suddenly covered by a shadow. When they looked up, they saw a bird flapping its wings overhead.

"Run!" they shouted, knowing it would be game over if a bird caught them, but the bird was bigger and faster, and it did manage to catch them all.

The first group of seeds lost.

The second group ended up in a city of stone. They, too, could not set up camp underground because the ground was simply covered in too many rocks. They tried to slip between the rocks to rest, some of them even able to reach the soil to get some water, but when the sun was high up in the sky, the rocks became hot as coals. Soon, the seeds could not stand the heat. They didn't want to get burned, so they decided to give up, calling out to the wind to carry them away and bring them back home.

The second group of seeds lost, too.

The third group landed in a thorny village. The thorny vines were plants, too, so they were friendly and gave the seeds a warm welcome. They even shared their water with the seeds. At first, the seeds were fine, and they thought that they had a good chance of winning the contest after setting up camp underground, but the thorny vines were bigger than they were, and they easily blocked the sunlight, which made it impossible for the seeds to cook their food. The seeds tried to push the thorny vines aside to make room for themselves, but the vines were just…too thorny. The seeds ended up getting hurt from all the sharp thorns.

"There's no way we can get the thorny vines to move," the seeds said. "And we can't survive without sunlight. We have to leave."

By the time they managed to make it out of the thorny village, though, they were already covered in cuts and too tired to move. They gave up, and the wind came and took them away.

The third group of seeds was out of the contest as well.

Only one group remained - the fourth group, which landed in the meadow. The ground was soft, so they were able to easily set up camp underground. There was enough water and sunlight, too. They might as well have found paradise. Needless to say, the fourth group made it through the week. By then, they had also become so used to their new home that they didn't want to leave, so the wind left them alone. They stayed in the meadow and grew into new plants, making a garden of their own.

The fourth group of seeds won the contest.

The people who listened to this story liked it, but they did not quite understand what it meant, so Jesus had to explain the lesson.

"The seed is the word of God," he said. "Some people are like the wasteland who only hear the word of God but do not understand or find room in their hearts for it, so wicked people, like the birds, can easily take the seeds away from them, and they forget they heard anything at all.

Some people are like the stone city. They listen to the word of God and try to understand it, but they do not really put it in their hearts, and when times get hard, they push the word of God away.

Other people are like the thorny village. They also listen to the word of God and try to understand it, but they get drowned in their worries, choked by their fears, and distracted by so many other things that the word of God becomes lost.

Finally, there are the people who listen to the word of God, understand it, and keep it in their hearts, just like the good ground. In them, the word of God finds a home and grows, spreading goodness and happiness."

Jesus had another story, this time about a farmer. Like the gardener, he was also good with plants, and he had a field that yielded a good harvest every year. Because of this, though, there were people who got jealous of him, and one night, one of them came in and planted weeds in his field. When the farmer saw the weeds, he sighed in dismay.

"Now, my field is ruined," he thought.

"Why don't you just remove the weeds, sir?" the farmer's assistant asked.

The farmer shook his head. "The weeds are too close to the wheat so we might end up pulling out some of them, and that would be even worse. We'll just leave them alone."

A contest began between the weeds and the wheat. "Now that we are here, let us see who will grow taller and last longer," the weeds said.

Some of the weeds did end up growing as tall as the wheat or even taller, but it did not matter when harvest day came. The farmer harvested all of the plants in the field, then he and his assistant separated them, storing the wheat so that it could be made into flour later on and throwing the weeds into a pile to be burned because there was no more use for them.

"So, too, will the good and bad people be allowed to live together," Jesus explained. "But at the end of their lives, the good people will receive their reward, and the bad people will have their punishment."

Finally, Jesus told them the story about the mustard seed. This mustard seed was among the smallest of seeds in the herb garden, so the other seeds made fun of him.

"He is so small that he will surely grow into a small plant, too," they said, laughing.

The tiny mustard seed felt sad, but he did not lose heart. Yes, he was small, so he could not play with the other seeds as much as he wanted. He could not even eat as much as they did. Still, he decided to focus on himself instead of comparing himself to others and grow at his own pace. So what if he still ended up being small when he was all grown? Even then, he would be grateful for the sun and the breeze and the rain and live as best as he could.

The tiny mustard seed did grow little by little in the herb garden. Soon, he became as tall as the chives and the parsley, surprising them.

"How did he grow so tall when he was so tiny?" they wondered.

The mustard plant did not know either, and he was even more surprised when he grew even taller, surpassing the mint.

"Hey!" the mint complained. "You never said you could grow so tall."

As the mustard continued to grow, the other herbs in the garden no longer complained or made fun of him. They all just admired him for his growth, and when he ended up being one of the tallest plants in the garden, turning into a small tree, they all cheered for him.

"You did well, mustard," they said. "We're proud of you for having come so far."

The birds were happy for him, too, and rested in his strong branches, so the mustard plant became very happy and proud.

Jesus explained this story to the people. "If you have the seed of faith in your heart, even if it is as tiny as a mustard seed, as long as you take care of it and never lose it, then it will grow and become stronger, and you will become stronger, too, and give strength and faith to other people."

The Missing Sheep

Do you know how many blankets you can make in a year from the wool of one sheep? As many as six small, fuzzy blankets!

During the time of Jesus, there were plenty of sheep in Israel, so there were also many shepherds enduring the hot sun and the cold winds just to take care of their sheep. Sometimes, they got bored and sometimes, they fell asleep counting their sheep. Sometimes, they faced danger, too, with many hungry wild animals lurking nearby. And what do shepherds get in return? Just a bit of money to get by.

Still, Jesus understood shepherds, who held a special place in his heart from the day he was born, and he told plenty of stories about them.

One of the stories Jesus told was about the shepherd and the thief.

Once, there was a shepherd with a beautiful flock of sheep who loved him dearly. They were so beautiful and healthy that a man who lived in the same town wanted to steal them.

"I'm sure I can make a lot of money selling those sheep," he thought.

When night came and the sheep were back in their pen and the shepherd had fallen asleep inside his house, the thief came. He climbed over the fence and grabbed the nearest sheep. It was too heavy for him to carry, though! Alarmed, the other sheep began to bleat, and the light came on inside the house, so the thief had no choice but to leave the sheep behind and run, thinking he would try his crime again another time.

The next night, the thief had a plan. During the day, he had watched the shepherd closely. Now, he dressed up just like the shepherd, then he climbed over the fence.

"Come with me, my sheep," he said, trying to sound like the shepherd as he opened the gate from the inside.

But the sheep would not move.

"Come on," the thief urged. "Don't you know that the grass tastes better at night?"

Still, the sheep ignored him.

The thief did not know it, but the sheep were speaking among themselves, laughing at him.

"Who does this man think he is, climbing over the fence of our pen?" they said. "He looks so funny wearing the same clothes as our shepherd. And what is with his voice? Is he coming down with a cold?"

No matter how much the thief tried to get the sheep to follow him out of the gate, they paid no attention, knowing he was not their shepherd. The thief had no choice but to give up, and he did not dare try to steal the sheep again.

"What is the meaning of this story?" the people asked Jesus.

"Only a thief enters the pen of sheep through the fence and not the gate," Jesus answered. "Even if the sheep don't know this, they know their shepherd well, and they will follow only him. I am the good shepherd. I know each one of my sheep, and they all know my voice. Other people may have tried to steal and trick my sheep, but my sheep will only listen to me. Thieves scare the sheep, hurt them, and try to destroy them, but a shepherd gives his sheep life as I do. Through me, all my sheep will live long, prosperous lives."

Jesus also had a story about a shepherd who once hired a man to look after his sheep for him.

"I am going away for a few days," the shepherd said. "So I will leave my sheep in your care. Look after them well, and I will pay you a good sum of money when I return."

Then he bid goodbye to his sheep and left.

The next day, the hired man led the sheep to the nearest pasture, which did not have the best grass. The hired man did not care. He just didn't want to walk far.

The sheep wandered far in search of good grass, and some of them ended up getting lost. Some of them also ran into another flock.

To the hired man, all the sheep looked the same, so he just brought back the nearest sheep he could find and did not bother to look for those that were missing.

On the second day, he took the sheep out to pasture again, but again, he did not pay much attention to them, finding his job boring. In the evening, however, something exciting happened. A wolf appeared, eyeing the sheep.

"Wolf!" the man screamed, then he ran away as his sheep scattered around him. He only came back for them in the morning, not caring that there were fewer of them than before.

When the owner of the sheep finally returned, he was disappointed to find that he lost so many sheep. Some of the sheep in the pen were not even his.

"What happened?" he asked the man he hired.

"A wolf attacked," the man answered. "So we all ran away, and some of the sheep got lost. But what was I supposed to do? Fight off the wolf and end up getting hurt?"

The shepherd was too sad to say anything.

"I would be sad, too," one of Jesus' listeners said after hearing the story. "But I'm also not sure I would have been brave enough to fight a wolf just to save my sheep."

"To a hired man, sheep are just animals that are not worth risking his life for," Jesus said. "But to a good shepherd, his sheep are his children, and he will face danger and risk his life to protect them. In the same way, I am ready to give up my life for my flock of sheep."

Jesus had another story about a good shepherd, this time one who owned plenty of sheep - one hundred of them, in fact.

Most of the sheep were pure white and clever, but there was one with gray wool that was not too bright, so the others liked to make fun of him. One day, while at pasture, they decided to play a little trick on him.

"Have you heard about the golden clover?" the white sheep asked the gray one.

The gray sheep's eyes grew wide. "There is a golden clover? I thought they were all green."

"Of course, there is." The white sheep laughed. "It's just very rare. In fact, it only grows at the bottom of the ravine over the hill. Not only is it rumored to be the most delicious clover, but it can change your wool into any color."

The gray sheep was amazed. "How do you know this?"

"Because a bird told us," they replied. "We'd go there ourselves and get some, but you know our shepherd does not want us wandering far. Still, we think he'd be very happy if someone found the golden clover. We bet it can be sold for plenty of money, too."

The gray sheep became even more interested. He knew the shepherd complained about money a lot. Maybe if he had lots of money, he would not sigh and frown so much but smile and sing more.

He looked at the shepherd, who was currently busy trying to free a sheep whose wool had been caught in a thorny bush. Now was his chance to slip away, and he was sure the shepherd wouldn't worry. After all, he lost his way all the time but always found his way back. He would be back before the shepherd knew it.

However, the gray sheep did not know that the ravine would be too deep. He jumped in but could not climb back up. Worse, he could not see any sign of the golden clover.

"Maybe I fell into the wrong ravine," he said as he sighed. "Why do I always end up doing the wrong things?" The gray sheep began to cry. "Now, the shepherd will never find me. Maybe he won't even look for me because I always get lost."

At that moment, the shepherd was actually already looking for the gray sheep.

"Where could that one have gone again?" he wondered.

He looked everywhere but could not find the gray sheep. As the sun started to set, he hurried to bring the ninety-nine sheep back to their pen, then he grabbed a lantern and went back out to the pasture.

"Where is he going?" one of the ninety-nine sheep asked. "Is he really going to leave us? What if someone steals us?"

Even the shepherd's neighbor was confused. "Don't tell me you are going back out to pasture when you have just returned," he said. "Isn't it too dark?"

"I'm still missing one sheep," the shepherd replied. "I have to find him no matter what."

"One sheep?" The neighbor sighed and shook his head. "Why worry so much when you have ninety-nine left?"

The shepherd did not care about what his neighbor thought. He did not care about anything else but finding his missing sheep. With a lantern in hand, he checked behind every bush, rock and tree and even went to the surrounding pastures, calling for his lost sheep.

The gray sheep who was at the bottom of the ravine heard the shepherd's voice calling for him, and he started bleating loudly and excitedly to let the shepherd know where he was.

"There you are!" the shepherd shouted triumphantly when he saw his missing sheep. "You must have been so scared, but you're fine now. I'm here and I won't leave without you."

The shepherd climbed down the ravine and picked up the gray sheep. Climbing back up was harder with the gray sheep in his arms but he managed. He carried it around his shoulders as he walked back home happily.

"I'm so glad I found you," he said. "Next time, stay close to me, okay? Even if you are just one of my sheep, you are important to me. All of you are. You make me happier than any riches or gold."

The shepherd's words gave the gray sheep a warm, fuzzy feeling, and he promised that he would stay by the shepherd's side from now on and not go searching for the golden clover or anything else. He, too, had everything he needed.

"It is a beautiful story," the people said to Jesus after he had finished telling it. "But what does it mean, Lord?"

"In the same way that the shepherd was thrilled to find his one missing sheep, the angels in heaven also rejoice with me whenever one person turns away from his wicked ways and realizes that the word of God is the most important thing," Jesus answered.

He continued to preach and tell stories, gathering his sheep as any good shepherd would and seeking out the lost ones so that he could save as many of them as he could.

The Vineyard Workers

S heep and grapes may not have much in common based on how they look, but just like sheep, grapes are hard to grow and take care of, and there were many of them, too, during the time of Jesus, hanging from vines all over Israel to provide both food and drink. Jesus spoke about himself as the one true grapevine with his faithful followers being the branches that he expected to bear fruit. He also told a story about a man who owned a vineyard and his workers.

Once, there was a man who had just bought a large and beautiful vineyard. The problem was that he had only a steward, the person in charge of managing the vineyard, but no workers to prune the branches, get rid of the bugs and make sure the soil was wet enough to keep the grapevines healthy.

"If I don't get workers soon, this beautiful vineyard will go to waste," the man said to his steward. "So I will make sure to find some tomorrow."

"And I will make sure they do their job well," the steward promised.

Early morning the next day, the owner went to the other vineyards to see if they had extra workers. Some of them did, so he invited those workers to come to his vineyard.

"You will find more work on my vineyard," he said. "And I will give you one silver coin at the end of the day."

"That sounds reasonable," they said. "And it is better than standing around doing nothing."

So the workers from the other vineyards came to work in the man's vineyard. However, there were not enough of them, so the owner went to the marketplace to find more. There, he found some men who were just yawning as they sat in their stalls, bored with no customers to entertain. There were also men who were looking for carts to pull and sacks to carry, and beggars who still had able bodies and men who were playing music or pulling off dangerous stunts just to get the people to toss them some coins.

The owner approached each one of them and offered them a job in his vineyard.

"If you would rather work in a vineyard and be rewarded a silver coin for your efforts, follow me," he told them.

Some of them went with him and began to work in the vineyard. The steward was pleased with them because they were quick learners and hard workers, but he still did not think there were enough of them.

"There are just too many cubits of land and too many vines," the steward told his master. "We need more pairs of hands to tend to each one."

After lunch, the owner went into town again and saw some men standing outside their houses.

"Are you busy?" he asked one of them.

The man shook his head. "I was going to take a nap but it's too hot."

"Then come with me and I will give you work," the owner of the vineyard said. "Of course, you will be paid."

A woman was sitting outside her house because she was already finished with her chores. The owner invited her, too.

"You look like someone who works hard," he said. "So why don't you work for me today and earn a silver coin? If you know some other women who also have nothing to do in their homes, bring them along."

The vineyard was full of workers now, men and women alike. The steward and the owner were both happy, but late in the afternoon, the owner decided to go out again.

"Are you still going to get more workers even though the sun will set soon?" the steward asked.

"I will," his master replied. "Because I have seen how happy my workers are to have something to do. I want to see if I can help even just a few more people."

The owner went back to the marketplace and saw a man who had just finished with his work at the butcher's stall. The man looked a little tired, but he did not seem happy.

"I still need more money so I can buy the medicine for my daughter," he said as he looked inside his purse. "But where can I get more work at this hour?"

The owner heard this and approached the man. "If it is work you're looking for, come with me, my friend."

The man was surprised. "Do you mean right now?"

"Yes, right now," the owner said. "There is still over an hour before sunset, after all, and while the sun shines, there is work to be done."

The man nodded. "Okay. I am grateful for whatever work you give me."

He and a few others who were finished with their jobs for the day but wanted more work followed the owner to his vineyard and they carried out the tasks the steward gave them.

Finally, the sun started to melt into the horizon, night creeping in. The steward rang the bell to let the workers know the day was done.

"Good work, everyone!" he said. "Now, gather yourselves so the master can pay you your wages for the day."

The workers gathered, and the owner stood before them. He called the man with the sick daughter and those he had hired before sunset first and paid them.

When they saw the silver coin, they were all surprised. "We only worked for a bit," they said. "Do we really deserve this reward?"

"Yes," the owner answered. "Take it and go."

The men left with smiles on their faces.

The owner called those he hired after lunch next, then the ones in the middle of the morning and finally, the workers from the vineyard who he had hired at sunrise. Unlike the other workers, when they saw their silver coin, they frowned.

"We were working from sunrise until sunset," they grumbled. "Yet you paid us the same amount as the ones who only worked an hour. It does not seem fair."

The owner frowned as well. "Did I or did I not offer you a silver coin for a day's work, and did you not accept it, saying that it was a reasonable amount?"

"It is," they said. "And if you had given the workers who only worked an hour a dime, we would not be complaining. But you gave them a silver coin, too, so you should give us at least three silver coins for our labor."

"So, you're telling me how to spend my money now?" the owner said angrily. "Are you being bitter just because I am kind?"

The workers said nothing.

"Go," the owner told them. "Take your coin and leave."

They left, still grumbling and with their shoulders sinking.

After telling this story, Jesus told his listeners, "The lesson here is that it is up to God to give blessings to everyone and that you must not complain or be envious if others have more. For a long time, the rich and powerful have always come first, but in the kingdom of God, the first will be last, and the last will be first. If you want to be at the top, you must first be at the bottom and serve everyone, just as I am not here for people to give me gifts, cook food for me, wash my clothes and shower me with attention, but to help other people and give them everything I have."

The Kind Stranger

A s Jesus traveled and preached the word of God, there were many people who tried to speak with him, wanting to impress him or ask him for advice. One of the most popular questions he got was: "How do we become good people so that God will bless us all our lives?"

"Obey the law passed down by Moses and follow God's commandments," Jesus would tell them. "Put God above all others and be good to your neighbor."

"But who exactly are my neighbors?" a lawyer asked. "Are they the people who live near me or those who I know and talk to everyday?"

Instead of answering this question directly, Jesus told the lawyer a story.

There once was a man who was traveling alone - just him and his horse and a long, rocky road ahead of them. They had to deal with a bit of rain and they had to go around some rocks that had rolled off the side of a mountain, blocking the road, but the journey was still pleasant, and with each day, they came closer and closer to their destination.

Unfortunately, though, one afternoon, the traveler and his horse caught the eye of a group of robbers.

"That horse looks strong and fast," one of the robbers said. "It must have surely cost a lot of coins and can be sold for even more."

"I'm more interested in the man's fine clothes," another robber said. "Even his sandals look well made."

The third robber touched his chin and grinned. "I have a feeling he has plenty of money in his purse and other fine things inside his sack."

The robbers decided to get them all. They blocked the road so that the traveler could not pass, smirks on their faces and weapons in hand.

"Please step aside," the traveler said to them. "You are scaring my horse."

"We are taking your horse," the leader of the robbers said. "And your purse and your sack and your clothes. Leave them and you can go."

However, the traveler refused. "You can take my purse, but I cannot give you my sack because it contains gifts for people who are waiting for me, and I cannot leave my horse that has been with me a long time."

The robbers laughed. "Did you think we were asking you? It seems you're not as smart as you look. I guess we'll just have to show you that we don't take 'no' for an answer."

The robbers surrounded the traveler so that he could not escape, then they pulled him off his horse and grabbed the sack off his back and the purse off his belt. They even pulled off his clothes and took the sandals on his feet.

"Help!" the traveler shouted as loud as he could. "Someone help me please! I'm being robbed!"

The robbers just laughed, knowing that no one would come to help.

"Did you really think someone would rescue you?" they said.

Then they kicked him and beat him with their fists until he could not stand. Only afterwards did they leave him alone, taking his horse and all his possessions and laughing about all the things they would do about all the money they had stolen.

An hour later, a priest came along, taking the same road. Even from afar, he was able to see the injured traveler.

"Oh my. It seems the robbers have found another victim," he said, then he looked around and pulled the reins so his horse could go faster. "I have to get out of here before they come back and take what I have as well."

Shortly after, a Levite also passed by. When he saw the injured traveler, he was shocked.

"Oh no! What have they done to this poor man?"

The traveler saw the Levite. He wanted to beg for help, but there just seemed to be something stuck in his throat. Still, he thought, "This man looks like he is my countryman. In fact, I think I've seen him before, working at the temple. Surely, he will help me."

However, the Levite shook his head. "This man has so many injuries he will probably not last long, so what use is it trying to help him? I will just help myself and reach the next town before dark."

So the Levite left.

The traveler wanted to cry. "Is there no one who is kind enough to help me?" he wondered.

As more time passed, the traveler began to shiver from the cold and from fear, both slowly and steadily creeping in. Soon, it would be evening, and not many people traveled at night because the roads were dark and there were wild animals who could attack them. Those same animals could easily attack someone as weak and helpless as him if he stayed by the side of the road. But what could he do? As much as he tried to move, he could not.

Just when it was about to get dark and he was about to lose hope, he heard the hooves of a horse approaching. Another traveler stopped beside him.

"Poor man," he said with a frown.

The injured traveler thought this man would not help him either since he looked like he was from another country, a complete stranger. Yet to his surprise, this stranger got off his horse. He knelt beside the injured traveler and applied medicine to his bruises then bandaged his cuts. He also gave him water to drink, washed him and put clothes on him, then he carried the injured traveler and placed him on his horse, bringing him to the nearest inn.

The next day, the stranger spoke to the innkeeper. "I have to leave and continue on my journey because there are people waiting for me to do business with them," he said. "But I am leaving behind a man in my room." Then he took out his purse and gave it to the innkeeper. "Here is some money for the room and for food and medicine for the man. Please take care of him until I return. If the money is not enough, I will be sure to pay you back whatever I owe you when I return."

The innkeeper didn't trust the stranger at first, but the money convinced him.

"Leave your friend to me and go on your way," he said with a smile. "I will make sure he is better by the time you come back."

After telling this story, Jesus asked his own question. "Who do you think acted as a neighbor to the injured traveler?"

"The stranger from another country," the lawyer answered.

"So go be a neighbor to anyone who is in need," Jesus said. "It does not matter which country they are from or whether they are friends of yours, people you have met before or complete strangers you never thought you'd run into. Help anyone who needs help. Be kind to them even if they cannot give you anything in return, even if no one sees or knows about what you are doing. God will know and he will be the one to give you a reward greater than riches or fame."

The Man Who Left Home

T oys you grew up with. Bedtime stories. Warm meals. Laughter and smiles. Hugs and kisses. These are the things that people remember when they think of home, that magical place which some people don't ever want to leave. Jesus, however, had a story about a man who couldn't wait to leave home. In fact, that is what the man did.

This man lived with his father in a big house on a hill where he was treated like a prince and had everything he wanted, even servants to make his bed, prepare his bath and meals and strap his sandals to his feet. Because of this, he didn't work, instead sleeping all day and feasting with his friends all night.

His older brother, on the other hand, was the opposite - responsible and hardworking - so he and his younger brother did not get along. He scolded his younger brother often, in fact.

"When are you going to grow up? Don't you think it's about time you helped father and me and tried to do something with your life?"

The younger brother laughed. "You are just jealous because Father loves me more and because I have so many friends while you have none."

Their father happened to overhear this conversation so he stepped forward. "I love you both equally," he said to his younger son. "And your older brother is right. You should start working and be more careful with the things you say and do."

The younger son frowned. "You two are so nosy, telling me to do this and that. If you can't leave me alone, then I will just get my share of the family fortune and leave. I've grown tired of this house anyway, and this country, too. I'd rather have a grand adventure somewhere far, far away."

It was his older brother's turn to laugh. "You, leave home? Do you even know how to put on your own sandals or put a saddle on a horse?"

Their father, however, was not even smiling, his expression as serious as when he did business. "If you really want to leave home, no one will stop you. Tomorrow, I myself will give you your share of the family fortune and you can go wherever you want and do whatever you think you must."

The next day, the younger son took his money, packed his bags and left home. He felt a little sad glancing back at the house he grew up in but he put up a smile as he looked forward to his grand adventure, heading to a faraway country.

He thought it would be all fun, so he was not ready at all for all the trouble. He got lost. He got into fights. He even ended up getting bites from bed bugs in a dirty room at an old inn and itchy rashes from using the wrong soap for his bath. Some of his money ended up getting stolen, too.

As for the money he had left, he gambled some away and wasted the rest on parties with strangers or things he didn't need, like an exotic pet or too many pairs of sandals. Of course, soon, he had nothing left at all.

At that same time, a famine spread throughout the country, and the young man found himself in an even worse pinch. The inn where he was staying closed down, and he was thrown out on the street. He tried to sell his things for money, but no one wanted fancy sandals now that food was getting scarce.

Tired and hungry, he turned to the people who used to feast with for help.

"Remember me and all the fun feasts we had?" he said to them. "Unfortunately, now, I have no more money for feasting, and I don't even have any more food or a place to stay. Can you help me?"

However, some of them looked at him like he was a stranger. "Aren't you from another country? We don't remember you at all."

Others didn't want to help him. "Can't you see there's a famine now? We need every bit of food we can get."

The young man had no choice but to do something he had never done before in his life and never thought that he would do. He looked for work. Because of the famine, though, work was scarce, too. The young man had to beg for someone to give him a chance.

"Please give me a job so I can have money so I can buy food to fill my empty stomach," he begged. "I will even work for food, and I will do anything."

"Anything?" a farmer asked.

"Yes," the young man answered.

The farmer nodded. "Very well. Many of my crops have died, but I still have some pigs. You can take care of them and in return, I will give you a loaf of bread a day."

The young man was thrilled. "Thank you! Thank you very much!"

Pretty soon, the man who never worked a day in his life was spending each day in the muddy fields with the pigs. He spent so much time with them he started smelling like them. The worst part, though, was that a loaf of bread a day simply was not enough.

"How I wish I had some meat with spices or some grilled fresh fish," he often dreamed. "Or even just four more loaves of bread, maybe with some wine or milk."

Once, he was so hungry that he eyed the husks of corn that the pigs were eating.

"Even the pigs are more well-fed than me," he thought. "I wonder how their food tastes like. If I eat some, maybe no one will notice."

He knelt down and picked up a handful of corn husks, putting them in his mouth. They were too hard to chew or swallow, though, so he ended up spitting them out, coughing.

"These corn husks are awful!"

As he coughed, tears leaked out of the corners of his eyes, and soon, he started sobbing.

"What am I doing so far away from home, working for a stranger who won't even give me enough food to eat?" he thought. "My father's servants never had to go hungry."

Then and there, he made a decision.

"I will go back to my country and my home. I know that I gave my father a lot of trouble and I said some mean words to him before I left so I do not expect him to forgive me. If he doesn't want me to be his son anymore, that's fine. I will go home anyway, beg for his forgiveness and ask him to let me work for him, even if it means taking care of his pigs or cleaning the kitchen."

The young man started the long journey home. Without any money to pay for a carriage, he had to walk for miles, eating whatever he could find along the way. Sometimes, his feet were so tired that he wanted to give up, but the thought of home, of a bed and a proper meal and a fire to keep him warm on chilly nights, kept him going one step at a time.

Finally, he got back to his country. Now, he just had to walk to his hometown. He did just that, and as soon as he arrived, he saw his father's house on the hill. His heart was filled with hope.

"Home," he whispered. "Just a little more and I'll be there."

His father happened to be looking out the window and saw him approaching. At first, he did not know the man was his son.

"Who is that stranger in tattered clothes covered in mud and why is he running to my house?" he wondered.

He was about to order his servants to go to the man and send him away, but as the man came closer, the master of the house recognized his younger son. Yes, he was thinner now, his cheeks skin and bone, but a father never forgot his son.

The master of the house ran out to meet his younger son. "My son!" He hugged the young man with tears of joy in his eyes. "I never thought I'd see you again. I should have never let you leave home."

"I should have never left home," the young man said. "Forgive me, Father. You gave me everything but I did not even try to be good, and now, I've even thrown away half your fortune. I do not deserve to be called your son anymore."

His father shook his head. "You are my son and this is your home. All that matters is that you have returned, so after you bathe and put on new clothes, we will have a feast to celebrate your homecoming."

When they entered the house, the servants stopped doing their chores and began to whisper.

"Who is that man who the master brought in? He smells like...like pigs."

"Wait. Is that the son who took half his father's money and left? Well, he looks like a beggar now."

"This is my son," the master of the house said to his servants. "You will serve him and treat him with respect. And tonight, we will have the grandest celebration of all so bring out the finest plates and the best meat and wine, and invite all of our neighbors and friends to come and celebrate with us."

"Yes, sir!"

The servants scrambled to do everything their master had told them.

Later, the older son came home from work. He was tired and looking forward to a quiet evening, so he was surprised to hear music coming from the house. He also saw many servants going in and out the front gates, some of them carrying lots of food.

"What is going on?" he asked one of the servants. "Has my father gone mad?"

"Your younger brother has returned," the servant answered. "Your father is throwing a feast for him."

The older son could not believe his ears. It was not that he couldn't believe his brother had returned. Somehow, he always knew it would happen. What he couldn't believe was why his father was celebrating. Had he forgotten that it was his younger son's decision to leave and that he took half the family fortune?

Furthermore, his father had never thrown him a feast, not even when he sealed a large business deal with a merchant.

Angrily, he started to leave, but his father saw him.

"My son!" his father called. "Come inside and celebrate with us. Your brother and all your friends are already waiting."

The older son clenched his fists. "Tell me, Father. Have I ever let you down or disobeyed you?"

"No," his father replied. "You have been the best son a father could ever ask for, and you are my pride and my joy."

"Yet you have never thrown a feast for me or showered me with this much attention as you are now giving your younger son who caused you so much pain and worry," the older son said. "I bet he's only home because he wants more money."

His father hugged him. "Please do not be angry, my son. All your life, I have given you everything, and you have never had to suffer. Everything I have is now yours. However, your brother has come home. I thought I'd lost him forever, but he is back home where he belongs. It is where we all belong. We are finally a family again, so let us celebrate."

The older brother hesitated, but he knew his father was right. This house was his home. He would not turn his back on it. It was his younger brother's home, too, and in spite of everything, they were a family. Maybe, just maybe, they could start over and be a happy family.

Final Words

Hey it's Ella Swan; I hope you enjoyed these enlightening Bible bedtime stories for kids. The only way for me to know what type of particular stories your child has enjoyed is by leaving an honest review on the product page, which will take less than 60 seconds of your time.

I will be able to create more tailored stories to your childs liking, and it will also help other parents discover this collection of amazing stories for kids!

Ella Swan :)